JACKY

Declan Furber Gillick

CURRENCY PRESS
The performing arts publisher

**MELBOURNE
THEATRE COMPANY**

CURRENT THEATRE SERIES

First published in 2023
by Currency Press
Gadigal Land, PO Box 2287, Strawberry Hills, NSW, 2012, Australia
enquiries@currency.com.au
www.currency.com.au

in association with Melbourne Theatre Company

Typeset by Brighton Gray for Currency Press.
Cover image shows Ngali Shaw and Guy Simon; photo by Tiffany Garvie.

Currency Press acknowledges the Traditional Owners of the Country on which we live and work. We pay our respects to all Aboriginal and Torres Strait Islander Elders, past and present.

A catalogue record for this book is available from the National Library of Australia

Contents

'Les blancs débarquent. Le canon!
Il faut se soumettre au baptême, s'habiller, travailler.'
('The whites disembark. Cannon fire!
You must submit to baptism, to dress, to work.')
Arthur Rimbaud, 1873

'Sexuality is to feminism what work is to Marxism:
that which is most one's own, yet most taken away.'
Catherine A. MacKinnon, 1982

'It is not to be doubted that a tract of land such as New Holland,
which is larger than the whole of Europe,
would furnish matter of advantageous return.'
Joseph Banks (addressing the House of Commons, Great Britain), 1779

'Settler Sovereignty is a constant performance
claiming to be an essence.'
Patrick Wolfe, *Traces of History*, 2016

'Colonialism presumes to prescibe whether the child
a woman bears in her womb becomes one of her own people
or one of her oppressors.'
Patrick Wolfe, *Traces of History*, 2016

'Any time you have to rely upon your enemy for a job,
you're in bad shape.'
Malcolm X, 1968

NEXTSTAGE

Commissioned through Melbourne Theatre Company's
NEXT STAGE Writers' Program, supported by the Donors,
Foundations and Organisations of our Playwrights Giving Circle.

With a $4.6 million investment by the Company and our Playwrights
Giving Circle, the NEXT STAGE Writers' Program has introduced the
most rigorous playwright commissioning and development process in our
history, setting a new benchmark for play development in Australia.

Thank you to Melbourne Theatre Company's Playwrights Giving Circle – its donors, foundations and organisations – for sharing our passion and commitment to Australian stories and Australian writers.

Louise Myer and Martyn Myer AO, Maureen Wheeler AO and Tony Wheeler AO,
Christine Brown Bequest, Allan Myers AC KC and Maria Myers AC,
Tony Burgess and Janine Burgess, Dr Andrew McAliece and Dr Richard Simmie,
Larry Kamener and Petra Kamener

The Ian Potter Foundation   NAOMI MILGROM FOUNDATION   THE MYER FOUNDATION   MALCOLM ROBERTSON FOUNDATION   THE UNIVERSITY OF MELBOURNE

Production supported by Craig Semple and the Trawalla Foundation.

Photo: Sydney Morning Herald

DECLAN FURBER GILLICK is a multidisciplinary artist from Mparntwe (Alice Springs) and a proud Arrernte man with Irish-Australian heritage. His practice spans writing, theatre, poetry, music, rap, film, television and visual arts. Declan will be making his Melbourne Theatre Company debut with *Jacky*. Other credits include *Scar Trees* (Ilbijerri Theatre Company) and *Bighouse Dreaming* (Melbourne Fringe Festival). He is currently working as part of a First Nations writing team to adapt Melissa Lucashenko's novel *Too Much Lip* for television. *Bighouse Dreaming* was awarded the Green Room Award for Best Independent Writing and Best Ensemble, Melbourne Fringe Awards for Best Performance Work and Best Writing, Melbourne Festival Discovery Award and Best Emerging Indigenous Artist. In 2018 he took up a residency as part of Melbourne Theatre Company's Next Stage Writers' Program. He has also worked with Melbourne Theatre Company's First Peoples Young Artist Program. Declan completed a Masters of Writing for Performance at the Victorian College of the Arts in 2017.

Greg Stone and Alison Whyte in rehearsal for MTC's production of JACKY. *(Photo: Tiffany Garvie)*

Dramaturg Jennifer Medway and Playwright Declan Furber Gillick in rehearsal for MTC's production of JACKY. *(Photo: Tiffany Garvie)*

Ngali Shaw in rehearsal for MTC's production of JACKY. *(Photo: Tiffany Garvie)*

Ngali Shaw and Guy Simon in rehearsal for MTC's production of JACKY. *(Photo: Tiffany Garvie)*

Director Mark Wilson with Alison Whyte and Greg Stone in rehearsal for MTC's production of JACKY. (Photo: Tiffany Garvie)

Director and Dramaturg Mark Wilson in rehearsal for MTC's production of JACKY. (Photo: Tiffany Garvie)

Playwright Declan Furber Gillick in rehearsal for MTC's production of JACKY. (Photo: Tiffany Garvie)

Guy Simon in rehearsal for MTC's production of Jacky.
(Photo: Tiffany Garvie)

Alison Whyte in rehearsal for MTC's production of Jacky.
(Photo: Tiffany Garvie)

Guy Simon and Ngali Shaw in rehearsal for MTC's production of JACKY. *(Photo: Tiffany Garvie)*

Greg Stone in rehearsal for MTC's production of Jacky. *(Photo: Tiffany Garvie)*

Greg Stone and Guy Simon in rehearsal for MTC's production of Jacky. *(Photo: Tiffany Garvie)*

I am of the Arrernte people, Arrernte Country
I am a guest on Wurundjeri Country
I continue to make my intentions known to this country and to its custodians
I continue to show gratitude and respect to this country and to its custodians
I work to stay in right relationship with this country and its custodians
I seek to understand and to make myself understood
I seek to show respect and I seek to make a contribution
Before too long I will return to my home country

For my dad

In memory of Galmahra, the guide
(also called Jackey Jackey)

Jacky was first produced by Melbourne Theatre Company at the Arts Centre Melbourne Fairfax Studio, on the lands of the Boon Wurrung and Wurundjeri peoples of the Kulin Nation, on 22 May 2023, with the following cast:

KEITH	Ngali Shaw
JACKY	Guy Simon
GLENN	Greg Stone
LINDA	Alison Whyte

Director, Mark Wilson
Set Designer, Christina Smith
Costume Designer, Emily Barrie
Lighting Designer, Matt Scott
Composer & Sound Designer, James Henry
Intimacy Coordinator, Amy Cater
Voice and Text Coach, Matt Furlani
Assistant Director, Joel Bray
Dramaturgs, Jennifer Medway and Mark Wilson

This work was commissioned by Melbourne Theatre Company's Next Stage program.

CHARACTERS

JACKY

KEITH

LINDA

GLENN

SETTING

Here.

Now.

NOTES ON INTERPRETING THE TEXT

A forward slash (/) at or near the end or beginning of a line indicates an interruption or overlap in dialogue.

A space or spaces between lines suggests a moment, pause or breath for the actor.

A dash (—) alone as dialogue should be interpreted and played as a silent action.

A full stop at the end of a line or paragraph of dialogue suggests a particular finality or emphasis.

[Square brackets] indicate that a word or phrase is not spoken aloud by the actor.

SCENE 1: APARTMENT

Music plays as the audience enters the theatre.

JACKY *sits alone on a lounge in a clean, well-arranged, tasteful apartment. He wears a well-fitted button-up shirt with some of the top buttons undone; smart pants, smart shoes. A smart jacket is hanging somewhere in the apartment. Some mail and a plastic bag of takeaway food sit beside him. It's been a long day.*

As the audience enters, JACKY *eats from the takeaway container, looks through his phone and flicks through his mail.*

SCENE 2: THE WORLD'S MY YABBY

Molly O'Brien's Irish Pub.

A front bar, a sports bar, a TAB. A television or two. An Irish flag, an Australian flag and an Aboriginal flag.

JACKY *and* KEITH *enter with beers.* KEITH *has a rugby bag slung over his shoulder. He is in the middle of an animated yarn.*

KEITH: 'The world's my oyster.' Fucksat mean, anyway? What the fuck does that even mean? 'The world's ya oyster.' He kept on sayin' it: 'You can do anyfin, Keif. You can do anyfin' dese days—tha world's ya oyster'

You know how he talk eh—Ol' Milky Balls—Laila was laughin' at him an' all, real quiet way

'Keif, bud! You gotta git dat education! Thass ya ticket! Thass your ticket outta here, Keif! Ya git dat education and the world's ya oyster!'

Laughter.

I said 'Oi Milky—no oysters out 'ere, bud; not in our river. Just yellowbellies, yabbies and dead cod. And a bit of run-off from the mines. Maybe the world's my yabby, Milks,' I said. 'Maybe the world's my gammon, shrivelled-up little yabby!'

Laughter.

JACKY *laughs.*

He just walk off, ay, like he does. You know how he walk, ay!

KEITH *demonstrates.*

JACKY *laughs.*

JACKY: Jeez, I forgot you're a funny little bastard, ay. Milky's right, but: education, bruss. That's your ticket. Can't get nowhere without it

KEITH: Yeah, yeah. Ay, what kinda pub's this? Is it a blackfullah pub or what?

JACKY: Irish

KEITH: True? Well how come they got the flag up? And how come they got these blackfullahs on the wall?

JACKY: This is Molly's. Molly O'Brien's Irish pub; it's where I worked when I first come down

KEITH: So the Irish are down with the mob, ay? Must be! Got the flag up an' all. Or was that you when you worked here? You woulda told 'em, ay! Full told 'em: 'Oi, if youse are gunna have that flag up … and *that* poxy flag up, youse gotta have the real flag up.' Represent, ay brother!

Nah, s'good to see ya. Fark, how long it been, anyway? Me and Laila was tryna work it out—and Mum. She always talkin' 'bout you, ay! 'Jacky got a nice place and a good job in the city, Jacky went to uni. When Jacky comin' home? You should be more like your brother Jacky.' Fark. How long since you been home, anyway?

JACKY: Keith

KEITH: They got a TAB in here? Where can I smoke? You got a smoke? /

JACKY: / *Keith!*

KEITH: What?

JACKY: Shut up for a minute

KEITH: Righto, righto

JACKY: Here's your Myki

KEITH: Whassat?

JACKY: For the trains and buses and that. Electric ticket

KEITH: Aww yeah, yeah, I know. Like when I come and seen ya in Sydney

JACKY: You gotta keep it topped up

KEITH: Yup

JACKY: With money.

KEITH: Yup, yup

JACKY: I chucked twenty on it for ya

KEITH: Mad

JACKY: You're welcome. Here's ya keys

KEITH: Oi, these mob got schnitzels or what? Got a fullah starvin' over here!

JACKY: Keith! Listen up. Here are your keys. Screen door, wooden door. I keep 'em both locked. I put 'em on this to go round your neck

KEITH: So who you livin' with? Blackfullahs or what?

JACKY: Nuh

KEITH: Whitefullahs?

JACKY: I'm not livin' with anyone. Got my own place

KEITH: What, just you?

JACKY: Yup. Near here. Block of flats just up the tram line. Good spot. Been there a couple years now. I got you campin' on the couch

KEITH: On the couch?

JACKY: It's only one bedroom. I'm not gonna make you pay rent or bills to start off with

KEITH: Rent? What, you own it or somethin'?

JACKY: No, I'm renting. For now

KEITH: But what—you gunna buy it?

JACKY: Maybe.

KEITH: Where'd you get the money to buy a house?

JACKY: It's just a flat. I'm just lookin' into it, that's all. But for now I pay rent. And it's not cheap. So once you get your apprenticeship transferred, you can chuck in too. Laila said you got some references?

KEITH: Ay?

JACKY: Notes. From your old bosses

KEITH: Aw, yeah, yeah, got 'em somewhere. In my bag there

JACKY: And you got any interviews or trials lined up?

KEITH: Ay? Nah, nah, not yet. I will soon, but

JACKY: What about your apprenticeship certificate? So you can transfer over?

KEITH: Yeah, for sure. In my bag. You want another beer?

> KEITH *has finished but* JACKY *has barely touched his.* KEITH *strikes a boxer's stance and announces loudly:*

Lllllllllllllet's-a-get-ready to aah-rrrrruuumbllllllllllllllle!

JACKY: / Keith!

KEITH: What?!

JACKY: Shut up! Bruss, you gotta rein it in a bit. This isn't the mish and this isn't the bush and this isn't home. Okay? Things are different down here. Pull your head in

KEITH: Yeah … I am. What? I thought these mob are down with blackfullahs?

JACKY: You can't come here and run amok like you do back home. Mum and Laila told me the kind of shit you been up to. It's not gunna fly here. Okay? If you're livin' with me, you're gunna have to follow a few rules

KEITH: Like what?

JACKY: You think I been down here runnin' my mouth, gettin' on the piss, causin' a scene? No. I'm on a good wicket in this town, bruss. Got my life in order. I'm takin' care of business, lookin' after myself. Doin' Mum and my old man proud. Alright? It's a good way to be.

KEITH: Okay. Okay, Jacky. I get it. Loosen up, bruss. I'm just havin' fun. Okay, I get it: play it cool; no runamok freaky blackfullah shit from Keithy-Boy, I get it. I'm all good, bruss, I got this.

So, what—you got a woman?

JACKY: You need to get your interviews lined up as soon as possible and get that apprenticeship transferred to a new bakery. There's heaps of bakeries down here. And plenty of Baker's Delight ones. Are you gunna stick with Baker's Delight?

KEITH: I dunno

Yes! Yes, I'll talk to 'em!

JACKY: Good man.

KEITH: I'm gunna chuck a bet on

JACKY: No, you're not

KEITH: What? My horse is racing

JACKY: Nah, we're goin'

KEITH: Naw, I was just gunna chuck one bet on. Just one!

JACKY: I got an appointment in a bit with the bank

KEITH: What for?

JACKY: Talk about gettin' a loan. Then I'm working tonight. And first I gotta show you my place. So let's go.

KEITH: What you doin' for work? Mum said you been doin' culture stuff, dance stuff

JACKY: Yeah, a little bit. Part time

KEITH: Part-time Jacky

JACKY: Got a thing next weekend, actually

KEITH: Where? What for?

JACKY: I don't know exactly. I ran into this woman the other night who got me the job here at Molly's; she works for this recruitment agency. But they're putting on some community event in a park. Culture and food and dance. Anyway, she said to come perform

KEITH: Ay, reckon you can get me some of that stuff too? That'd be mad. Some of the brothers was doin' culture stuff again up around home last year. For a bit. I been practisin' didge an' all

JACKY: We'll talk about it later

KEITH: Boom! That's it. Things gunna work out deadly. I should call up Milky Balls and tell him: oi Milks, turns out the world *is* my oyster after all! And I didn't even need to 'git dat education'

JACKY: Come on, I gotta get movin'. Don't forget your bag

> KEITH *has his arm around* JACKY.

KEITH: Nah, s'good to see you, my brother! S'gunna be mad livin' wit you in the city!

SCENE 3: WIN-WIN

A lively cultural event in Melbourne's suburban parklands; families, food, music, cultural performances. JACKY *has performed and is getting changed. He has his shirt off and some paint on his body.* LINDA *is nearby attending to the members of her choir. She approaches* JACKY.

LINDA: Brilliant. Loved it. Everyone loved it

JACKY: Sorry I was a bit late

LINDA: No stress

JACKY: Had a pretty good audience

LINDA: Culture in the Park. Our third one. Gets bigger every year

JACKY: Your work puts this on?

LINDA: Well, I put it on, really. I bully them into it paying for it. They take the credit

JACKY: Isn't Segway just like a recruitment agency?

LINDA: Segway is a community-based employment and vocational training organisation, thank you very much. And this is part of our

Communities Program. Been a few changes since you graced our foyer. I've been trying to take us in a new direction

JACKY: Clearly. A choir?

LINDA: Ah, yes! The Segway Women's Community Choir; we'll be on shortly. Just waiting on a couple of them to arrive—

You sticking around for a bit? Help yourself to food; those curries are to die for

JACKY: You haven't seen a scruffy little black larrikin wandering round have you? I told my brother to come down

LINDA: Your brother?

JACKY: Keithy-Boy Cooke, everybody's favourite bloody liability. He's staying with me

LINDA: Is he? Here for a while?

JACKY: We'll see. He's been gettin' himself in a bit of trouble up home. Mum and our sister sent him down, wanted me to straighten him out

LINDA: He working?

JACKY: He has been, yeah. He's got this baker's apprenticeship that Laila and I set him up with. He's meant to have transferred it down here, but he just lacks—I dunno—motivation.

LINDA: Well, if you need help getting him into work, you know where I am. I bet he loves stayin' with you

JACKY: Oh yeah, he loves it; no rent, no work, Xbox and Uber Eats on the couch. Where are those curries? If he is here, that's where he'll be, loading up a plate

Nah, he's a good kid. Funny. I do love him. My apartment's just small. And he takes up a bit of space, if you know what I mean

LINDA: Oh, I do. My husband and I are separated, but we've been living under the same roof

JACKY: Didn't even know you were married

LINDA: No, well, normally I try not to bore people with the tedious minutiae of my personal life. He's been living in our converted, semi-detached extension thing for over a year. And it's not quite detached enough, if you know what I mean. Sick of the sight of him. But the settlement's nearly done, thank christ, and he's finally rented his own little flat.

She notices people arriving.

Fatima! Hullo Usman! Head down, Fatima, I'll be there shortly, the
ladies are waiting

Hey, how'd you go with your apartment?

JACKY: Oh

LINDA: Weren't you looking at buying it?

JACKY: Yeah

LINDA: Well?

JACKY: Bit of a false alarm

LINDA: I thought the owner was desperate to get rid of it. You said it
was a steal

JACKY: It is

LINDA: You were meeting with your bank?

JACKY: I did. They won't give me a loan

LINDA: You're working, aren't you?

JACKY: Yeah. A lot. And I've got a fair bit saved. But all my work's
casual; freelance; 'gigs'. That sort of thing

LINDA: I thought if you'd left Molly's, you must have finished that
business degree? Gotten something permanent?

Did you finish your degree?

JACKY: —

LINDA: You didn't finish it? So what are you doing for work?

JACKY: I went back to … what I was doing before you got me the job
at Molly's

LINDA: Jacky

JACKY: I know

LINDA: I thought you were done with it? I thought the whole plan was
to get some formal qualifications and develop your a career

JACKY: I know; I was meant to leave it behind in Sydney, get a straight
job, build a profession

LINDA: Financial security?

JACKY: Financial security, get out of that lifestyle and invest in my
future. I know. That was the plan. It's tricky to make the transition.
I've been doing it a long time. It's easy money. Good money. I'm
good at it

LINDA: I'm sure you are. So that's where your savings come from

JACKY: Yeah, I mean, I have a good income, especially when I have a
few regulars

LINDA: But the bank wants to see a permanent employment contract

JACKY: Exactly. Regular, registered, consistent income. They won't lend me money

LINDA: I can get you a contract. Easy

JACKY: What, another bar job?

LINDA: No, no, a real contract. At Segway. I've got all these traineeships to fill

JACKY: In what area?

LINDA: Wherever. They're funded as part of the Communities Program. They're designated as 'culturally and/or linguistically diverse'. Some are specified as 'Indigenous'. One of them's yours if you want it

JACKY: Are you serious?

LINDA: Deadly serious. I could just stick you in the finance department. Part time, full time; probably full time for your loan, yeah?

JACKY: Aren't there other people, like, going for the traineeships?

LINDA: Honestly, I haven't had many applicants. I actually thought of you when I got them funded, but I imagined you'd be off and away on your career by now, smart young guy like you

There's funding for professional development too; suited to your field. For you it could be support to finish your business degree. Financial support

JACKY: Segway would pay me to study?

LINDA: I told you: Segway has changed. We're not just rushing people through a cert four in retail and shoving them into dead-end jobs any more—we've got a vision. We've got outreach services: after-school care, arts and crafts, cultural days like this, language classes; community building. We're working with a local Indigenous org, too

JACKY: Really?

LINDA: Sisterhood, they're called. Grassroots group. They were just here.

JACKY: They run programs for women in prison, don't they?

LINDA: Support their families, help them into jobs when they get out. Impressive. Headed up by Aunty Dawn … ?

JACKY: Aunty Dawn Langhorne

LINDA: That's it. You know her?

JACKY: Well, not personally. But I mean, I know who she is. Everyone does. She's a Langhorne. Everyone knows that name.

LINDA: I swear I saw them over by the—

Anyway, I'll introduce you. They saw your performance. Loved it.

JACKY: And they're working with Segway?

LINDA: Partnership launches officially in the new financial year

So. Wanna get involved?

JACKY: You hardly know me

LINDA: I know enough. More than enough. Jacky: motivated, handsome, enterprising young Aboriginal man; student of business, strong rental history, sense of family responsibility, culturally engaged. Significant savings. 'Small business owner'

Interview done.

JACKY: It'd be a pretty big favour

LINDA: Maybe for you. Not for me. In fact, you'd be doing me a favour by taking the position. The board need to see that the money's being put to good use, or they won't give me any more. It's win-win.

I mean, what's your rent?

JACKY: A lot

LINDA: And where does rent go? Into somebody else's nest-egg

JACKY: Yeah

LINDA: Financial independence is what you want

JACKY: I sort of told my landlord I couldn't go through with it

LINDA: When?

JACKY: This morning

LINDA: Call him back. What does your bank need to see, exactly?

JACKY: Evidence of full-time work, weekly income—they want to see a permanant contract

LINDA: I could start you as a full-time casual immediately. And you'd have a permanant contract in the new financial year when the traineeships get renewed. In the meantime, I'll just write a letter—a very official letter—saying that you work for me full time and I'm preparing your permanent contract to start on the first of July.

Honestly, Jacky, after what I've been through with this settlement; if you've got even half a chance to get into the market and get your own place while you're young, you'd be insane not to take it.

There's Nasrin—I should get back

JACKY: Maybe I should call my landlord again

LINDA: Do it now. And top your savings up. You got someone that could go guarantor? Your mum?

JACKY: You gotta be joking

LINDA: What about your dad?

JACKY: He's got property

LINDA: There you go

JACKY: But we don't talk

LINDA: Get some good clients. A few regulars. The more you have in the bank, the less you'll be asking to borrow

JACKY: You sure all this is … I mean, it's no hassle for you?

LINDA: Jacky, I promise you it's a piece of cake; like I said: it's win-win

Linda's gone.

SCENE 4: WHAT KIND OF BLACK ARE YOU?

JACKY *and* GLENN *are in a nice Airbnb apartment.*

JACKY *has on a smart casual suit, with the jacket off.*

GLENN: I've never done this before.

JACKY: That's okay, hun. A lot of guys haven't. I see a lot of guys and it's their first time with someone like me

GLENN: Someone like you?

JACKY: Is it your first time with a call boy? A rent boy? We can just sit and talk. We don't have to do anything in particular. We don't have to do anything, we can just sit and talk. Or cuddle or …

Would you like a drink?

GLENN: It's … I'm not … I'm not that hard. I haven't been getting that hard lately. It's just … I wanted to let you know.

JACKY: That's fine. It happens with a lot of guys.

GLENN: I know it's fine. I'm not apologising. I just wanted to point it out before—

JACKY: Before what?

GLENN: Before you said something

JACKY: What did you think I was going to say?

GLENN: 'What's wrong?'

JACKY: But nothing's wrong, babe

GLENN: I know. That's why I said it. Is something wrong now?

JACKY: I don't know. Is it?

GLENN: I don't know.

Can I see your cock?

JACKY *lowers his pants, facing* GLENN.

JACKY: There you go. What do you think?

GLENN: It's nice

Really nice.

JACKY: Thanks

Silence.

So, did you want to show me yours or—?

GLENN: What? No

JACKY: Okay. No rush. Just take your time. Would you like me to … leave this thing out or put it away?

GLENN: I don't know. I don't know what I want. I thought I wanted this.

JACKY: Okay. It's okay to not know. Look, I'm just gunna put these back on, for now, okay? And we can just sit and talk. About what you want. Or about nothing. Or about something else altogether. What do you do for work?

GLENN: I work for myself. I deal in records and hi-fi gear. Rare vinyl.

Oh; I—here—I've got the money. I didn't know when you wanted me to … sorry, I should've /

JACKY: / It's okay

GLENN: Sorry … here

He has cash.

JACKY: Hey …

You can just leave it on the table

GLENN: What did you say your name was again? Sorry. What's your name?

JACKY: Jacky.

You know:

[*Sings to the tune of 'Jackie', by B.Z. featuring Joanne*] Jack Jack Jacky

GLENN: Jacky.

Jacky, what kind of black are you?

Which kind of black are you?

JACKY: Which kind do you think?

GLENN: I don't know. It looks like a mix

JACKY: What kind of black were you looking for? Which kind of black did you have in mind?

GLENN: I don't know. I looked at a few profiles. A lot. I've been thinking about this for a long time. Wanting to do this. I decided to—I wanted to after I spoke to my—

My wife and I are—

Well, we aren't really—

JACKY: I get it

GLENN: Do you have … ?

JACKY: A boyfriend? Nah

GLENN: I guess this kind of work would make it difficult?

JACKY: People are open-minded. Lotta guys do it. Lotta guys do it and have boyfriends. Girlfriends. It's just work, you know

GLENN: Where are you [from]? I'm sorry, I know it's—it might be rude to ask. Where are you from?

JACKY: Up north.

Silence.

Is that the kind of black you were after?

GLENN: I don't know.

JACKY: It wasn't really, was it?

GLENN: I don't know. This all comes from something else. I've … I've talked to my therapist about it. My therapist decided; well, I decided; well, we both decided that during the divorce—see the divorce was because—well: lots of reasons

JACKY: It's always lots of reasons

GLENN: But I've got this thing—like—and it's like a fetish I guess, like—the therapist said it's like a kink, I suppose

JACKY: Black cock

GLENN: Yeah

Kind laughter.

JACKY: Don't feel so alone. I mean, join the club

GLENN: But not just that. It's like; I've watched so much porn. The therapist and my wife—and I—think I scrambled my brain. Like, I feel like I've given myself brain damage or something and, like, I can't fuck my wife. I haven't been able to fuck my wife.

Well, I could do it. Like, I can do it. But I had to think about ...
porn. Images. Things I've seen. And it's like ... it was like putting
a screen on my wife's head and fucking her while I looked at a
computer—like I was watching porn. You know?

I felt like, like I might as well have put a computer screen on my
wife's head and just ... fucked like that and /

GLENN *is distressed.*

JACKY: / Hey ...

GLENN: It's messed up

JACKY: Hey ... it's okay. Hey. Glenn. It's okay. I'm happy to be here
with you and listen, you know?

GLENN: All I can ever ... think about. To ... get hard ... All I can ever
think about to feel anything ... is big black cock. And my wife.
Together. Like—her fucking a big black guy—and loving it—and
I know that's so fucked up.

JACKY: It's pretty common

GLENN: It doesn't matter, / I

JACKY: / It's really common

GLENN: It doesn't matter. I can't go on like that. Like I can't go on like
this. You know? It's ... porn and this obsession is ... it fucked up
my whole marriage. Like, what's it even about, you know?

JACKY: So was your wife not into it?

GLENN: A bit. In the beginning she was. Years ago. She's always ...
humoured me, I guess. But ... it doesn't go away. It doesn't ever let
up and it's just ended up like this wall between us

JACKY: So she wouldn't have wanted to come here with you?
I do that kind of thing
Would you want me to fuck her?

GLENN: No. Well. Yes.

JACKY: I still could. If she's into it

GLENN: She wouldn't be into it. She's over it.

JACKY: Fair enough. Plus, I'm probably not the right kind of black.
Well, come on. We both know what you're into. It's the 'black'
man. The big black man from out in the fields. The big strong negro.
The big strong negro, here to take your wife.

GLENN: Yeah

JACKY: —

GLENN: That's what all the porn is like

JACKY: That's what all the porn that *you* like is like.

GLENN: It's called cuckold porn

JACKY: I know

GLENN: I need to get my shit together. Get my life together. Need to get up out of this mess. Out of this rut. The divorce. You know? It's not—it hasn't hit me fully yet. You know?

JACKY: These things take time

GLENN: So I need to—I wanted to explore and see what … I wanted to—I need to see and understand and come to terms with some of the things I've been avoiding. And I've never been with a man; well, not for a long time. Since I was at music school. TAFE. And I've spent so many years fantasising about black cock and I just wanted to try it out.

JACKY: So what do you think? Is it going to do the job?

GLENN: You seem sensitive

Are you always like this?

Sensitive. Kind. You're listening. To me.

JACKY: This is your time

GLENN: But we get along, yeah?

JACKY: Yeah, we get along, for sure, babe

GLENN: How long do we have left?

JACKY: Forty-five minutes in the first hour. Then, if you want, we can take it into the next hour. I'm easy. We can do one or two hours. Price-wise, it'll depend what we do. The hour's one-fifty as a base rate. Then services are priced on top of that. Like, if we fuck—that's full service—that's three-fifty total. I'd do the second hour for a bit less if you had full service. Or you can get the full BFE.

GLENN: What's that?

JACKY: BFE? Boyfriend Experience. That's overnight, babe. I'm like your boyfriend. Till tomorrow. Normally you gotta book that ahead but I had a ten o'clock cancel and that was my last appointment. So you're it, babe. For the night. BFE is eight hundred. And we can do whatever

I just don't kiss. Alright?

GLENN: Can I see it again? I want to see it.

JACKY: Your money, babe

SCENE 5: THAT'S LIFE

JACKY *arrives home.*

KEITH *is playing video games on the couch.*

The apartment is a bit of a mess.

JACKY: I thought you were gunna put the rubbish out and do your dishes

KEITH: I done the dishes

JACKY: Then what are these?

KEITH: Huh?

JACKY: Then how come there are dishes on the sink?

KEITH: I done the ones from yesterday. Them ones is from today

JACKY: Fuck, you're useless, ay

KEITH: Ay, no need

JACKY: No need? You need to get your shit together and stop livin' in a pizza box

KEITH: Ay, don't talk about your apartment like that. You got a nice apartment.

JACKY: Did you call the bakery up home? To get your certificate?

KEITH: Yeah

JACKY: And?

KEITH: No answer

JACKY: No answer? How many times did you call?

KEITH: What you gotta hassle me for? You're worse than Laila. She called earlier, actually. Bubba Ruby said her first word

    JACKY *looks through Keith's phone.*

JACKY: What time did you call the bakery?

KEITH: I dunno, lunchtime

JACKY: Twelve? One?

KEITH: Yeah

JACKY: About one, ay?

KEITH: That's it

    KEITH *notices* JACKY *looking through his phone.*

Oi, that's private!

JACKY *unplugs the TV and game console. The video game's various sounds disappear.*

What the hell, Jacky, you fuckin' dog? What was that for? Plug it back in, you gammon prick! And get out of my phone

JACKY: You didn't call no-one about your certificate. You didn't send any emails. You didn't give your résumé to any local bakeries. You haven't even edited your résumé. You haven't fronted up at any of the local bakeries in person. You been here nearly a month and you're not payin' me any rent. You're eatin' Uber Eats three times a day on my account. You're drinkin' a six-pack every day and you've hardly been outside since you got here. Except to go to Molly's to throw money away on no-hope horses

KEITH: I had a win yesterday

JACKY: Good. Pay me some fucking rent, then. Did you call the bakery about your certificate or not?

KEITH: I'll get Laila to pick it up. Her work's next to the bakery. She knows them

JACKY: Laila has an eleven-month-old baby—your niece—whose father is in prison. She's gotta drive all the way into town every day to work at the community centre, then come back to the mish and look after Mum and Bubba Ruby, do Mum's medication, cook a feed, deal with everyone still fightin' after Nan's funeral—which she handled pretty much on her own—then she puts Bubba Ruby to sleep, then she gets up and does it all again. Why would she go and get your certificate?

KEITH: She's helping me

JACKY: Bruss you gotta learn to help yourself

Call them now. Call the bakery now and say 'Hi, it's Keith Cooke, I used to be the apprentice there, I need a transfer of my apprenticeship certificate so that I can get a job in Melbourne'

KEITH: I don't know the number

JACKY: Here. North-West Bakers' Delight.

JACKY *has* KEITH'*s phone.*

Now call 'em. Or what? Are you too shame?

Silence.

KEITH: There's no certificate

JACKY: What?

KEITH: They didn't give me one

JACKY: Why not?

KEITH: They fired me

JACKY: When?

KEITH: I dunno, after like two months. The boss told me get out and forget about my apprenticeship

JACKY: What for?

KEITH: No reason

JACKY: He fired you for no reason?

KEITH: I dunno, I was late sometimes. I couldn't get into town. I missed a couple of shifts. Okay, I missed a few

JACKY: What about the bike I got you?

KEITH: It broke.

JACKY: So why didn't you fix it?

KEITH: No money

JACKY: That's why you have the job

KEITH: The job was shit, anyway

JACKY: The job was shit? Me and Laila worked our arses off to get you that apprenticeship

KEITH: The boss was a cockhead. He was! You don't even know

JACKY: Life's full of cockhead bosses, bruss. You just deal with it. That's how it is.

KEITH: That shit gets all through your fingers. Little bits of like … in between your fingers and up your arms—

JACKY: Keith

KEITH: And up in your elbows and all in your arm hairs and all this shit, brah. Flour! Dough!

JACKY: Remember we said to you: 'Okay, you don't wanna go to school any more? Fine. What do you wanna do Keith? You wanna work at the community centre like Laila?' 'No.' 'You wanna work at the clinic?' 'No.' You wanna learn to be a teacher's assistant and work at the school?'

KEITH: Fuck that

JACKY: Exactly: 'Fuck that.' So what did we ask? 'What do you like? What are you good at?' 'I dunno, cookin'.' 'Okay, so maybe you wanna learn to be a baker?' 'Yeah, righto'

KEITH: But not every day, man! Every day in that flour! Sticky little bits of balls, and not just your arms, but on your face! And in your hair—like in my hair on my head, man. It's fucked. It's full fucked!

JACKY: Keith

KEITH: And four in the morning! You gotta get up at four a.m. I was startin' at five a.m., six days a week. And then they switch it up on you with no warning or nothing: last minute, you gotta do a night shift. On a Friday night! Start back at seven o'clock on Friday night and work till three a.m. What the hell is that?

JACKY: That's the job, Keith. That's the job of a baker

KEITH: Well that sucks

JACKY: Well that's life

KEITH: That's not life. I'm not here on earth to work my ring off all day and all night—'yes sir, no sir'—for some white boss who pays me twelve bucks an hour and looks at me like I'm gunna steal his car. He's not workin' for twelve bucks an hour

JACKY: That's apprentice wages. You were only a junior. You get more pay later, when you get better at it

KEITH: I was already better at it. It's a piece of piss. Machines do most of it anyway. The bread that me and the other apprentice made was just as good as the boss's. They sell 'em for the same price. The other apprentice was makin' the same money as me and she been there two years. I'm not dumb, bruss. It was a shit job

JACKY: No. It wasn't. It was a good job, actually. In fact, it was a career. You wanna eat and drink? You wanna have a roof over your head? You wanna have Xbox? You gotta work. Laila works. I work. Even Mum still works. You don't wanna finish school? Fine. But you don't wanna be some 'poor-bugger-me blackfullah', sittin' around the mish broke with your hand out like—

KEITH: Like who?

JACKY: It's good to have work, bruss. It's dignified. It gives you a bit of self-respect.

KEITH: You think that's how our mob lived? Ay? You think that's how our old people lived? Runnin' round middle of the night, makin' these little bits of twisty bread so whitefullahs can sell 'em to other whitefullahs and get rich? They'd be laughin' 'emselves silly if they seen that

JACKY: I'm this close to sendin' you home. Look at my place. It's filthy. The apartment didn't look like this before you got here.

I'm happy to give you a leg-up, bruss, help you get started; you know that. But you gotta take some responsibility. Personal responsibility. You gotta pull your weight. Laila's too busy to be chasin' round after you and Mum's too old to be stressin' out about your bullshit. It's time to grow up.

> *Silence.*

KEITH: Okay. I'll get a job. Doin' somethin' else.

> I will.

> I can get a job.

> I can, brah.

> Nah, look, true gawd, brah, I can get a job.

> I'll get it together, okay? I won't even play Xbox no more. Honest, brah. I'll get it together, brah, I will. I'll get a job

Don't send me back, brah. Alright? I like livin' with you. It's good. It's like school holidays, when you used to come back and stay at the mish

> Remember?

> Please, Jacky. I'm sorry

> *A few moments.*

> JACKY *is tidying, unpacking his bag.*

> *A few moments.*

> KEITH *begins tidying.*

Laila sent a video.

> Of Bubba Ruby talkin'.

> If you wanna see it

SCENE 6: ONLY TIME

Morning. Jacky's work Airbnb. JACKY *and* GLENN *are both in bed, asleep. Sunlight. Maybe bird sounds, a tram, a truck.*

JACKY *wakes and checks the time. He gets out of bed and into his pants. He puts on his shirt, leaving it open. He looks at his phone and continues getting dressed.*

GLENN *wakes.*

GLENN: Oh

JACKY: Yeah

GLENN: Oh, have we both—?

JACKY: Yeah

GLENN: Oh, I didn't mean to—What time's checkout? I didn't mean to / stay

JACKY: / It's okay, there's time

GLENN: Shit. I didn't mean to—

JACKY: Me neither

GLENN: What time is it?

JACKY: Quarter-to-nine

GLENN: Ah

JACKY: You late?

GLENN: Nah—well—I was gunna head out to the markets at King Lake, maybe. Sell records. Doesn't really matter if I don't go. Markets are—those markets are a bit hit-and-miss

JACKY: Are they?

GLENN: Hey look, I didn't mean for—I didn't think it was …

JACKY: It's okay

GLENN: I hadn't budgeted for—

JACKY: It's fine

GLENN: Because, well, just last week we had—I mean, last week we had two overnight sessions and /

JACKY: / It's cool, babe, it's cool

I didn't have any other clients; I would've had the same outgoings—just the overheads on the room. So I haven't lost anything

GLENN: Oh, okay

JACKY: Only time

GLENN: Oh, okay.

Do you have many other regulars?

JACKY: Nothing too serious. Last night I would have just been at home

GLENN: Me too

JACKY: So yeah. It doesn't make that much of a difference, really

GLENN: Do you have far to go?

JACKY: Nah

GLENN: Shout you an Uber?

JACKY: You're a sweetheart. All good—I'll stretch the legs

GLENN: So no full BFE fee?

JACKY: Don't worry about it

GLENN: You sure?

JACKY: Like I said, it hasn't cost me anything

GLENN: Okay

JACKY: Yeah. It's chill. All good

GLENN: Can I … can I get you a coffee at least? There's a … [place nearby]

JACKY: Yeah, for sure

> JACKY *leaves the room to use the bathroom.*

Chuck the kettle on. Make it a tea, though, ay?

> *He calls out.*

Hey, but since this is becoming such a regular thing, maybe we should set it up as a direct debit … ?

GLENN: Oh, okay

Milk?

JACKY: Nah, babe

> JACKY *returns.*

Just one less thing to worry about, you know. We get to have our sessions. The fee's capped. Comes out weekly. You don't have to think about it. Up to you. It's what regulars usually do. You've been enjoying our time together, yeah?

GLENN: Hey? Oh, yeah. Yeah, yeah.

JACKY: The cuckold stuff—the dirty talk—about how I fucked your wife and all that; that's working for you?

GLENN: Yeah. Yeah.

JACKY: Right kind of black?

GLENN: Uhhh—yeah

JACKY: Thought so

> *The kettle boils.*

> GLENN *gets dressed.*

> *He sings softly.*

GLENN: *Jack-Jack-Jacky*

GLENN *is about to make the tea.*

JACKY *pulls a lidded carry mug from his satchel.*

JACKY: Here, babe, chuck it in this

GLENN *makes the tea in the carry mug.*

Legend

GLENN *puts the cup on the table.*

JACKY *is finishing getting ready.*

Thanks, Glenn, you're such a darl

GLENN: You're welcome

JACKY *puts the lid on his carry mug. He is dressed smartly.*

You do some other kind of work, too? Sorry. None of my business

JACKY: I don't mind. I better make a move

GLENN: Yeah, yeah, same

JACKY: When you leave—

GLENN: Yeah?

JACKY: Would you mind just leaving this key in the lockbox by the door?

GLENN: Sure, sure

Oh. What's the code?

JACKY: You won't need it. You just pop it in, hang it on the little hook, then shut him up and away you go. These mob change the code all the time anyway

GLENN: Aw yeah

JACKY: Did you—did you make yaself a cuppa?

GLENN: Aw. Nah.

JACKY: Awright, babe. Gotta hit the frog-'n'-toad. Hey, good seein' ya

GLENN: Yeah, good seein' you, Jacky

Moment.

Hey, I think I will set up the payments—direct debit, like you said … if that's alright?

JACKY: Yeah, yeah, of course, babe. Too easy. Weekly? That's how I usually run it. I'll text you the details?

GLENN: Okay. Too easy

JACKY: Yeah, I reckon it's better that way. For both of us. You have a good one, ay?

JACKY *leaves.*

GLENN: Yeah. Have a good one

JACKY *returns.*

JACKY: Oh yeah—Glenn? Nine-thirty. They'll come and clean at nine-thirty

GLENN: Too easy

JACKY *leaves.*

GLENN *makes himself a cup of tea.*

He sings or whistles.

Jack-Jack-Jacky

SCENE 7: ASSET

Later. GLENN *has met with* LINDA *on her lunch break.*

LINDA: Can you believe that price? In that area? That's an absolute steal. Owner must be bankrupt or something.

Such a lovely young man. Cluey. And so well-spoken. Already showing himself to be a real asset. His brother's after some work too. Got him in this evening for a trial at that Irish pub down the road. You know—Molly's? Owners used to play in Sharon's band? Apparently he can cook a bit. And he goes there to have a punt, watch the football. Rugby.

Glenn?

GLENN: Sounds promising

LINDA: Yeah. Anyway. That's me. I haven't got too long. The board've sprung an urgent meeting on me at one. How were the markets?

GLENN: Oh, ah …

LINDA: Saturday? Saturday markets? King Lake this morning, isn't it?

GLENN: Oh, didn't really go

LINDA: Didn't go?

GLENN: Bit tired

LINDA: That's a shame. Nice day for it. Look at that sun. Would've thought you'd make a killing today

GLENN: Just been a bit busy

LINDA: That's good. What with?

GLENN: Oh, all sorts of stuff

LINDA: Good-oh.

You seen your accountant?

Your accountant. About your tax

GLENN: Oh

LINDA: The settlement, Glenn. The settlement on the house

The conveyancer has asked that you finalise your taxes

GLENN: I will. I'm sorry

LINDA: I need to know how much I'm up for

GLENN: I will take care of that. I'm doing it

LINDA: I need to budget

GLENN: Yep

LINDA: I want these renos done before Jill has the baby. Dad's will's nearly finalised. I'm the executor, remember?

GLENN: Yeah, of course, I—

LINDA: But once it's been split between all of us it's not exactly going to be a grand fortune

GLENN: No

LINDA: And I need you to—

What have you been doing?

GLENN: Sorry.

I'll get onto it.

I will. I'm sorry.

How is Jill?

LINDA: She's a moody little cow

GLENN: I bet

LINDA: But she looks divine. I'm seeing her tonight. It was her birthday

GLENN: I know

LINDA: On Sunday

GLENN: I know. I tried to … I left a message. Same number, yeah? She still got the same … ?

LINDA: She's so busy

GLENN: Absolutely, for sure. I can imagine

LINDA: I said to her the other day—you better not be screening my calls. Or I'll be screening yours when you need a babysitter

GLENN: I got her something

GLENN *takes out a vinyl record in a brown-paper slip.*

LINDA: Oh, good on you, Glenn. What is it?

GLENN: The Stones. *It's Only Rock 'n' Roll*

LINDA: Good one. She loves their hard rock and disco years. Not for me, personally

GLENN: Nor me. But she played my copy of *Black and Blue* to death. Remember she used to dance on the coffee table? Jagger and Richards co-produced that—

LINDA: 'The Glimmer Twins'

GLENN: Exactly. And, well, same with this one

LINDA: God, I can take the stones without seventy-four to—oooooh—

GLENN: Eighty-two?

LINDA: Spot on. Seventy-four to eighty-two. Although Billy Preston's keys are gorgeous on this

GLENN: Best part, really. Do you think you could … if you're seeing her tonight?

LINDA: Of course

GLENN: She's due in July, yeah?

LINDA: Mid-July.

Shit. I've really got to run. The board are really riding me at the moment

GLENN: There's a card there. Tell her happy birthday from me. When you see her

LINDA: I will

She handles the record.

She'll love this

LINDA *leaves.*

SCENE 8: INVESTMENT FOR THE FUTURE

That evening at Molly's. KEITH *is telling a joke over his beer.*

KEITH: And so these kids, they was chuckin' this boomerang round, awright? And they chucked it too far in the wrong direction: fut-fut-fut-fut-fut-fut-fut-fut smack!

Hit one of them old fullahs in the back of the head.

And you know what he said?

JACKY: —

KEITH: He turn around and he reckon: 'Oi! What Kung Fu that?'

And so that's how us blackfullahs invented Kung Fu!

JACKY: What the hell kind of joke is that?

KEITH: You get it? 'What Kung Fu that?'

JACKY: Yeah, I get. It's just stupid

KEITH: Naw, that's Brother Seanie's joke. Seanie Choolburra from up Townsville-way. Deadliest dancer. Funniest bloke! You know Brother Seanie Choolburra! Remember he used to tour round the schools and that? And played at the community centre in town. Even done that show out on the mish, man. 'Member Mum took us to see him when he come to the mish? Me, you, Laila … Nan even come

JACKY: That's right

KEITH: And she laughed so hard she spat her false teeth out on the stage, remember? And Sean come over and picked 'em up. And he reckon—what'd he say? He reckon—to Laila—he reckon, 'These yours, sis?'

JACKY: True ay!

KEITH: And Laila was screamin' with tears comin' out her eyes! And Mum was laughin' so hard she couldn't hardly breathe!

Laughter.

JACKY: I forgot all about that. Yeah. He is funny, Sean Choolburra

KEITH: He's still tourin' round. Got videos on YouTube and all

JACKY: What's the time? Got your uniform?

KEITH *takes out a branded polo shirt and holds it against his chest as* LINDA *enters.*

KEITH: How do I look, Linda?

LINDA: Very nice

JACKY: What you reckon, Linda, would you give him a run?

LINDA: All set, Keith?

JACKY: Can I get you a drink?

LINDA: Oh, no, I won't stay too long. Keith I've got some forms for you

She takes out some forms.

Responsible service of alcohol. Gaming license. Food handling and hygiene

KEITH: So I'm not just gunna be washin' dishes?

JACKY: You gotta start at the bottom. But they know you can cook a bit. So if you do your job, and you're reliable, you'll get a shot as kitchen hand, and they might trial you as a barman. But only once you do this training. So get the forms filled out, and don't lose them. Linda is paying for it all

LINDA: Well, Segway is

JACKY: As a favour to you; to us

LINDA: Don't mention it

JACKY: Hey I heard from my bank. They've given me conditional pre-approval on the loan

LINDA: That's great news

KEITH: So what, the bank just gives you money to buy the aparment?

JACKY: If I'm working in a permanant position like the one Linda's organised, they'll lend me money. They won't give me it. Plus you've gotta have savings

KEITH: And you got savings?

JACKY: Yeah

KEITH: How much?

JACKY: A bit

KEITH: What from?

JACKY: Working. Saving. Not betting on horses. Keith's a gambling man

LINDA: Is that right?

KEITH: It's not gambling if you know how to win. I was gunna chuck a bet on now, actually

JACKY: You start work in three minutes

KEITH: Just a little tiny quick one

JACKY: Get your shirt on and get out the back

KEITH: Fine

> KEITH *finishes his beer as he puts on his shirt.*

Oi, thanks heaps for your help with this, Linda. I just been sittin' round on Jacky's couch since I got here

JACKY: Yeah, spending my money

LINDA: Just doing my job. Really

KEITH: Gotta let him save for that apartment

> KEITH *is ready to start work.*

JACKY: Lookin' good, bruss

LINDA: Hey, good luck Keith. Enjoy your shift

JACKY: And don't fuck around

> KEITH *is gone.*

> *A moment.*

I told Mum about the new job, the traineeship

LINDA: Did you? And was she pleased?

JACKY: She started bloody crying. I told her about the apartment, too

LINDA: Already?

JACKY: I just said I'm looking at it. Didn't say it was confirmed. But I'd just got that pre-approval. And my broker reckons it's looking good. So I told mum it's looking good

LINDA: What did she say?

JACKY: I sort of had to explain to her: if I bought an apartment here, it wouldn't mean I'm gunna live here like forever. When I come back home, I'll just rent it out, get tenants in to pay off the mortgage. It's a place to live, but really it's like an investment for the future, you know?

I think she also just just wishes I was home more

LINDA: —

JACKY: The mob up there—my family; it's sort of tricky for them to grasp stuff like this. They live week to week, hand to mouth. The idea that I might have like a real career and own an apartment in the city—it's kind of foreign. Abstract. I mean, up until recently it was pretty foreign to me too

Hey how was your 'emergency meeting' with the board?

LINDA: Fine. Yeah, fine. Nothing big. Just some changes for the new financial year. Boring structural stuff. Fairly routine.

JACKY: You know, no-one in my family knows what I do for work. Well, I think my sister might, but she never says anything. It's gunna be nice not to have to lie any more

SCENE 9: I THOUGHT OF YOU

JACKY *and* GLENN *are in the work Airbnb.* GLENN *has a beer.* JACKY *has a cup of tea.*

GLENN: You know how you're usually the one in control—
JACKY: Yeah
GLENN: You normally penetrate me?
    Well, tonight I … I was wondering if I could have a go at being in control. I wanted to maybe try being the one that … does the penetrating
JACKY: You wanna top me?
GLENN: Can I? Could I? How do you feel about that?
JACKY: I feel great about that
GLENN: Yeah?
JACKY: Yeah. Top, bottom; I'm easy, babe. I'm what's called 'versatile'. Explore what feels good. That's what we're here for
GLENN: Great
    Oh. And Jacky: I'd really like it if … Do you think you could call me 'Daddy'?
JACKY: You got it, Daddy
GLENN: Hey, you like the blues?
JACKY: What kinda blues?
GLENN: Any kinda blues
JACKY: Some
GLENN: Yeah?
JACKY: Yeah … some blues I like
GLENN: Who? Who do you like?
JACKY: Aw, I dunno. I'm not a big aficionado. Like you, Daddy
    I just, I like the sound, you know?
GLENN: Sure, sure. Of course.
    But you got a favourite era, or, like, region or even instrument?
JACKY: Nah. Aw, well, I guess I like B.B. King
GLENN: Sure, sure! B.B. King. The Man. The Master. Yeah, B.B.'s the guy. Four notes—that's all he needs. He'll hold your attention for half an hour with four notes on the blues scale. The B.B. King

Box—that's what they call it. It's why he owns the blues. Especially major blues scale
    If you don't understand the blues, you don't understand nothin'.
    If you don't understand the blues, you don't understand shit
        What kind of music did you grow up with?
JACKY: Well, Dad was never big into music. But with Mum's side, country
GLENN: What kinda country? Bluegrass? Honky-tonk?
JACKY: Country-and-Western, I guess
GLENN: Ah … cryin' music
JACKY: Ay?
GLENN: Country-and-Western's cryin' music
JACKY: That's all the mob ever listen to back home on the mish: Charlie
    Pride, Merle Haggard, Patsy Cline, Hank Williams. 'So Afraid of
    Losing You Again'. Charlie Pride. That's Mum's song

> JACKY *sings several lines from the song. He sings well, mimicking Charlie's twang.*

GLENN: Oh boy. Yup. That's cryin' music alright
JACKY: Yeah, that's Mum's music
GLENN: Well, you know where that comes from?
    The blues
JACKY: Really?
GLENN: Sure, sure! It all comes from the blues. Everything does
JACKY: Everything? Everything comes from the blues?
GLENN: Trust me. Jazz? Blues. Rock and Roll? Blues. The gospel? Gospel
    choirs? That's just the Bible plus the blues. You know Sister Rosetta
    Tharpe? Whoo boy, get yourself a good dose of Sister Rosetta, a nice
    glass of good cognac and—sorry, well a nice cup of … tea /
JACKY: / I get it /
GLENN: / And siddown and have a nice long listen to Sister Rosetta.
    Trust me. You gotta know the blues. You gotta understand the blues.
    If you don't know the blues, you don't know shit about shit, Jacky
        I, uh, I got you somethin'
JACKY: Oh?
GLENN: Yeah. It's … it's nothin' really, it's just …
JACKY: What is it?
GLENN: Well, I'm a … I sell records, you know?

JACKY: Sure, sure

GLENN: So, it's, it's nothin' really … I just … see … I'm a blues man. I love the blues. I really love the blues, you know?

JACKY: Hadn't noticed

GLENN: Yeah! And I just love the origins, the early days. Mississippi Delta, and the juke joints … before the juke joints. Folk music, you know? All the old folk ballads. And the working songs.

Anyway. I just … like I said, it's nothin' but I … got you this

GLENN *takes out a record in a brown-paper slip cover.*

JACKY: What is it?

GLENN *hands it to* JACKY, *who slides the record out.*

Thank you, Glenn. Glenn, this is very thoughtful.

Thank you

GLENN: Do you have a player?

JACKY: Yeah, yeah I have one

GLENN: Great!

I, uh, I hope you like it. Like I said: I'm a blues man, and, well, I just saw this and for some reason I thought of you

SCENE 10: THE BLUES

KEITH *is busy completing the preparation of a home-cooked meal in Jacky's apartment, which is clean and tidy.*

JACKY *enters with a new (second-hand) record player.*

KEITH: You got any more plates?

JACKY: What are you doing?

KEITH: You got one plate and you got one bowl. And until I give you them glasses, you only had one glass

JACKY: Did you cook somethin'?

KEITH: Smell lovely, ay! Siddown

JACKY: What's goin' on?

KEITH: How was work?

JACKY: Good. Did you make—?

KEITH: Lubbly lamb roast! Gravy there. Potatoes there. Peas there

JACKY: You made this?

KEITH: Pumpkin. Even done the carrots how Mum does 'em

JACKY: You did this?

KEITH: Fuckin' oath

JACKY: What for?

KEITH: Sunday roast

JACKY: It's Thursday

KEITH: Ya welcome

> JACKY *sets up the record player as* KEITH *transfers the meal to the table.*

JACKY: Fuck. Smells awright ay

KEITH: Smell deadly ay! Proper lubbly roast 'ere, true gawd! Pumpkin, potatoes, gravy. Even—there, look

JACKY: Mint jelly

KEITH: Course! Can't have lamb roast without mint jelly. Mum go crook for her mint jelly

Whassat?

JACKY: Record player

KEITH: You don't have any records

JACKY: A bloke at work gave me one

KEITH: What work? Segway? Like a present? That's pretty weird

JACKY: Why?

KEITH: Gettin' presents for blokes you work with. What is it?

> JACKY *stands and handles the record.*

JACKY: *African-American Folk Songs. Volume 1. Mississippi Delta*

KEITH: What's that?

JACKY: I think it's like … the early blues

KEITH: Alright, here, siddown. Have a glass o' Coke. I got Coke there. No sugar. Diet Coke just for you!

> KEITH *pours* JACKY *Coke into a beer glass then picks up his phone and dials. He puts the phone on loudspeaker as it rings.*

JACKY: What are you /

KEITH: / Shhh, just wait

JACKY: Who are you calling?

KEITH: Laila

JACKY: Why?

The phone rings out.

KEITH: We was gunna talk, that's all. They was gonna have roast too

JACKY: Who?

KEITH: Laila and Mum. And Bubba Ruby. They didn't have roast on Sunday like normal cos no money, so I said you mob should do it on payday—Thursday—and I'll do it on Thursday too. I'll make a roast and I'll surprise Jacky and we'll call you mob and we can have it together. But then Laila called this arvo and said she had to take Mum to the hospital

JACKY: What? Why?

KEITH: I dunno, her new kidney medication wasn't workin' or somethin' and her breathing was like a bit weird

JACKY: Why didn't they go to the clinic at the mish?

KEITH: There's no clinic at the mish

JACKY: Since when?

KEITH: They had to borrow a car and go into town

JACKY: What about Laila's car?

KEITH: Broke down. So Laila turned the roast off. She said to call her later when we're about to eat and we can have a yarn anyway

JACKY: So is Mum alright now?

KEITH: I dunno

Silence.

Do you reckon she's gunna die?

JACKY: No.

I mean, one day, yeah

KEITH: But soon? Laila reckons she is

JACKY: No she doesn't

KEITH: She full does

JACKY: She's full of shit

KEITH: She was sayin' on the phone the other night

JACKY: She's makin' a big deal out of nothing

KEITH: She's the one living with her

Silence.

I'll try Laila again in a bit.

Who gunna say grace?

It's Sunday roast. Someone gotta say it.

Can't be me. I made the feed

JACKY: Okay. Um … okay. Thank you … for this feed—

KEITH: This *deadly* feed

JACKY: This 'deadly' feed that we are about to eat. Thanks for family and friends

KEITH: Don't forget 'the lord'

JACKY: Who's sayin' this grace?

KEITH: Just don't forget the lord, that's all!

For Mum

JACKY: Thanks to the lord for this deadly feed, for family and for friends and for … colleagues; for us having a roof over our heads and … for my new job. And for Keith's. And yeah, blessings on this meal

KEITH: Thank. Thah. Laaawwwd!

> *They eat.*

JACKY: Far out

KEITH: Told ya

> *They eat in silence.*

Oi may as well chuck that record on

JACKY: Yeah?

KEITH: Yeah. I wanna hear this 'early blues' thing

> KEITH *looks at the cover.*

'Side one: Working Songs from the Chain Gangs and Plantations'

> JACKY *places the record on the turntable.*

What's the plantations?

> JACKY *drops the needle.*

> *A Traditional Black American work song plays.*

> *The brothers eat and listen.*

Ay. That's deadly

> *They LISTEN.*

JACKY: Yeah.

Yeah, it's deadly.

SCENE 11: SEEING SOMEONE

LINDA *and* GLENN *have met for a drink and to sign the final settlement papers.*

LINDA: 'The sector's under pressure, Linda. You know that. Your program's been a good little experiment, but in this economy, it's just not realistic any longer.' What a bunch of fuckwits.

    She's signing the papers.

And get this—I then had to go straight off and see my trainee—that young guy I promised a permanant contract to? He'd already told his mother that he had a new full-time job and was about to buy that property.

    She slides the paper across the table

GLENN: So did you tell him?

LINDA: Sign there. Dotted line. No, I could barely look him in the eye. Anyway, fingers crossed I won't have to. Never thought I'd say this, but thank god for the minerals sector

GLENN: How do you get in touch with the minerals sector?

LINDA: One of the board members knows a couple of reps from major groups. Threw me a bone. All done? Finally. Cheers

GLENN: And they want to invest in a recruitment agency?

LINDA: They want to donate to Indigenous community programs

GLENN: Segway's not an Indigenous community program

LINDA: Well, we sort of are now

GLENN: In what sense?

LINDA: Well Sisterhood is. And we're partnered with Sisterhood. And plus several of our traineeships are Indigenous positions. Which means that with a bit of the right framing the Communities Program qualifies

GLENN: That's lucky

LINDA: God, it'll be a lot of money if we get our hands on it. We can do language classes three times a week, Culture in the Park twice a year. Maybe a minibus; I could take the women's choir on tour! And the board can shove their wage freeze. If we land this, I'm giving myself a real promotion

GLENN: That'll help with the renos

LINDA: Just gotta nail these two prospecting events—the second one's a bigger thing, a formal sort of dinner, with families invited. I emailed you an invitation, actually

GLENN: Thanks

LINDA: No pressure.

The girls at Sisterhood—the little grassroots outfit—they're still a bit iffy about it all

GLENN: I wonder why

LINDA: Sorry?

GLENN: Well. Mining money? Maybe it doesn't—I don't know—gel with their principles

LINDA: And what have you been doing with yourself lately, Glenn?

GLENN: Not much

LINDA: Not much?

GLENN: Playing a bit of guitar. Got a few new songs. Had a jam this morning

LINDA: On a weekday?

GLENN: With some of my old mates. Pete—you remember Dirty Pete?

LINDA: I do recall Peter, yes

GLENN: Danny D. Dan said to say g'day

LINDA: Getting the band back together?

GLENN: Maybe, maybe; we'll see. Just been enjoying playing again, really. The blues, you know? Those old blues

LINDA: That's nice

GLENN: Yeah. Yeah it is.

And … uh … well—

LINDA: —?

GLENN: Well, I guess I've been … seeing someone

LINDA: Seeing someone.

Seeing someone as in—?

GLENN: As in, yes, as in, seeing someone … regularly and … frequently

LINDA: In a romantic—?

GLENN: That's right, yes, seeing someone in a romantic capacity. Regularly.

LINDA: Didn't take you long

GLENN: Are you seeing anybody?

LINDA: No. No, I'm not.

GLENN: Right

LINDA: Well, nothing serious. Nothing that warrants ... disclosure

What's she like?

GLENN: Different

LINDA: Different?

GLENN: Different, yeah. Really different. It's early days, I guess, in the relationship

LINDA: Relationship

GLENN: But I feel really excited. I didn't think I'd move on so quickly. I'm seeing things in sort of a ... new light

LINDA: I bet

GLENN: Anyway, I just ... I thought I should let you know

LINDA: Younger?

GLENN: A little

LINDA: Mmm

GLENN: A little bit younger, yeah

LINDA: Do you think that's wise?

GLENN: 'Wise'?

LINDA: I mean it all sounds wonderful, don't get me wrong. It's just that it wouldn't be the first time that a man your age ... came out of a marriage, came into some money and ah—got involved with a younger woman

GLENN: You don't know what you're talking about

LINDA: No, of course not

Silence.

And how does she go with it all?

GLENN: Sorry?

LINDA: How does she find the whole 'big black cock' thing? Or haven't you mentioned that yet?

Haven't you told her that that's a role she'll have to play for you? Or is that just something you used me for?

GLENN: It's not like that

'Used'? ... Used you for?

LINDA: In your puerile, mysoginistic, racist little fantasies

GLENN: Linda. Please, could you keep it down?

LINDA: Year after year after /

GLENN: / Jesus Christ

> GLENN *stands.*

What is wrong with you?

LINDA: What's wrong with me? Nothing. I just hope she knows what she's getting herself into

GLENN: Not that it's any of your business; and not that it's even something you can probably even understand

LINDA: Try me

GLENN: But this relationship isn't actually anything like that. In fact, it isn't actually anything like what you think it is. Okay?

LINDA: What's it like then?

SCENE 12: RELATIONSHIP

GLENN *and* JACKY *are in the work Airbnb.*

GLENN: Do you ever feel 'used'?

JACKY: Do I feel used?

GLENN: Yeah

JACKY: Not really

GLENN: Not really?

JACKY: I mean, if that's how a particular client likes to 'play'—if that's their kink, then yeah. If that's what the play itself is actually about, then yeah. That can be hot. But generally no

GLENN: One time I remember she said that it was like having something done to her. Is this ever like having something done to you? Like when I tied you up? Or when I call you names? Is that / okay or is that … ?

JACKY: / Babe, this is an exchange. A relational, consensual exchange.It has a framework. It has boundaries. Trust. If there's something I'm not comfortable with, I don't have to do it. Like in any healthy relationship.

GLENN: You know, you're not like any other Aboriginal people I've ever met. Certainly not any men. You're different.

JACKY: In what sense?

> *Laughter.*

GLENN: I don't know, you just are.

How did you end up … why do you do this?

JACKY: Why do I do this? Like, *this*?
      Why not?
      We have fun, don't we?
GLENN: Yeah, yeah
JACKY: It's a pretty good gig. Choose my own hours, set my rate. And
      I mean it is sex. I do like sex. I can't do it forever. No-one can. It's
      not exactly a secure career. Lenders won't touch me. But it's been
      good for a time. I kind of like being my own boss, you know?
GLENN: Me too
JACKY: I did start something else recently
GLENN: Oh yeah?
JACKY: Yeah. A straight job. In my field. Just casual for now.
GLENN: Right
JACKY: Yeah. I'm hoping it will lead to something a bit more secure.
      There are some things I need to start thinking about for my future.
      I want to get back to uni, too. Finish my study
GLENN: That's smart. Good on you. I never got a real tertiary
      qualification. It's made things pretty challenging. My wife—my
      ex-wife; she was the main earner for us

      So what, at some point do you plan to stop seeing clients?
JACKY: I mean, at some point, yeah. Well, most of them, anyway

      Hey, how's your daughter?
GLENN: Good. Oh my god. Beautiful. I saw her. Yeah, I saw her. Finally.
      She's so amazing. She's so big. Her belly. It's so big. Incredible.
      I've never seen one up close like that. Wow
JACKY: Beautiful
GLENN: She's not my daughter. Technically. Well, she is, I mean,
      I raised her. With my ex-wife. Together. And I love her.

      I just don't see her so much these days, since the start of the divorce.
      Even less since I moved out
JACKY: That must be hard
GLENN: It is.
      It is hard. It's really fuckin hard.
      Distress.
      You know?

JACKY: Yeah

GLENN: I mean, come on! I raised that girl from a child. Her mother worked round the clock, worked weekends, had her career. And good on her. I don't begrudge her that. I was happy to do it. Her father wasn't around. He's never been around. I cooked, I did school runs, I took her to swimming lessons, I went to parent–teacher night. I taught her to play guitar. She's a musician now. Her mother and I did it together, you know? We raised her together. And now, what, because her mother kicked me out, it's like I've disappeared off the face of the earth

I'm sorry

JACKY: It's okay

GLENN: I'm sorry. It's a really difficult thing

JACKY: Give it time

My sister just had a baby

GLENN: Did she?

JACKY: Yeah

GLENN: Whoa. Congratulations

JACKY: Thanks. Well she's nearly … nearly a year old, actually

GLENN: Oh, okay. What's her name?

JACKY: Ruby. Ruby-May

GLENN: That's a really pretty name

JACKY: Isn't it? We call her Bubba Ruby

GLENN: Bubba Ruby-May!

JACKY: I've never seen her

GLENN: Oh …

JACKY: Yeah. I haven't met her yet

GLENN: How come?

JACKY: Just … just haven't been home … in a bit

I mean I've seen photos and on FaceTime and that. She recognises my voice. But I've never … met her yet. Properly. Got my brother stayin' with me at the moment though

GLENN: Yeah?

JACKY: Yeah, crashed on my couch

GLENN: What does he do?

JACKY: Fuck all

Laughter.

Nah, he's alright. A friend and I just got him a job. It's good for him. He's been running amok up home. People up there, they've got nothing. Keith didn't get the same opportunities I did, growing up. My dad's white. I went to college in Sydney. Keith's dad ... well, Keith didn't get a lot of guidance. He doesn't have a lot of focus. Just raw energy.

Kids like Keith, they get into all sorts of shit. Mum stresses out, worries about him gettin' on the gear

GLENN: Right

JACKY: Sorry

GLENN: No, no

JACKY: Sorry, it's not your problem. I'm fine.

GLENN: No, no. I'm happy to listen

JACKY: Nah ... Keith—Keithy-Boy Cooke—

GLENN: Is that what you call him?

JACKY: That's what he calls himself!

> *Laughter.*

He's okay. He's a good kid. He just ... He wants to live his life, you know?

GLENN: Who doesn't?

SCENE 13: MY HOUSE

KEITH *and* JACKY *arrive home to the apartment together.*

JACKY: Keith, you're imagining it

KEITH: You really don't think Linda was actin' weird?

JACKY: No, I don't

KEITH: Well I do

JACKY: Based on what? You hardly know her

KEITH: The way she was laughing and smiling with them blokes in suits

JACKY: 'Laughing and smiling'? Yeah, really weird, Keith. Absolute lunatic behaviour

KEITH: Does Aunty Dawn know those blokes?

JACKY: Aunty Dawn isn't the boss of Segway and she doesn't know every last little thing, and every last person does she?

KEITH: I reckon them girls from Sisterhood thought something weird was going on

JACKY: For god's sake, Keith. It was just a pizza night. For community building and networking. There's another event next Saturday night. And in fact, Aunty Dawn is going to do a Welcome to Country and some of the Sisterhood girls are doing cultural performances. And so am I. You're invited again. But if you think it's all some big racist conspiracy, then feel free to sit it out

KEITH: I never said that. I just reckon there's something about Linda and Segway that's … fake

JACKY: Is the job and the training they got you fake? Is your pay fake?

KEITH: Bruss, fuck that job

JACKY: Here we go. What's wrong with the job now?

KEITH: I went through my payslips the other day. I reckon they paying me wrong. I done twenty-five hours last weekend and I reckon they paid me for twenty

JACKY: I reckon your count's probably out

KEITH: The hours are shit. I never even know how long I'm gunna go till. Or what time I'm startin'. They do the roster like one day before. And they call me on my day off

JACKY: It's bar and hospitality, bruss. That's just how it is

KEITH: They reckon they can just tell us dishies to come in and go home whenever they want

JACKY: Well hurry up and get your training done for bar so you can work front-of-house

KEITH: I done it weeks ago. Piece of piss. Did the RSA and the gaming-licence thing in like half a morning

JACKY: So why aren't you working front-of-house?

KEITH: Why do you think?

JACKY: Of course. Cos you're black. 'Boo hoo poor blackfullah Keith'. Nice try, but I used to work there too, remember? On the bar

KEITH: Yeah, that's different

JACKY: How?

KEITH: We get treated different. We do. All your new work friends and them blokes in suits too; the way they look at me, the way they talk to me. We get treated different. You don't see it

JACKY: That's cos it's in your head. People see you how you see yourself. You wanna be a victim? You wanna live like a victim? People gunna treat you like a victim. You wanna be a poor-bugger-me blackfullah? That's how people are gunna treat you

Silence.

KEITH: Why do you think Linda's so excited to have you at Segway?

JACKY: Because I do my job, I'm good at it, and I don't whinge about it. Because I'm not stuck in the past and I don't walk around feeling sorry for myself. And because I'm her friend

KEITH: Yeah—her only black friend

JACKY: She has heaps of black friends

KEITH: Yeah, African and Indian and shit. Not 'black'-black.

JACKY: What about Aunty Dawn and Sisterhood?

KEITH: They're not her friends

JACKY: What are they, then?

KEITH: I don't know, like, clients?

JACKY: And so what am I?

KEITH: I dunno—her token black?

JACKY: Fuck off

JACKY: People like Linda love blackfullahs like you

JACKY: Fuck you, Keith

KEITH: Runnin' round smilin', introducin' you to everyone: 'oh this is Jacky, our new Indigenous trainee, one of our shining stars'

JACKY: I said drop it, Keith

KEITH: There was somethin' weird goin' on tonight

JACKY: If you say 'weird' one more time—

KEITH: I don't know why you trust Linda

JACKY: Linda works hard, she does good work, she cares about community, and she's my friend. She's done me some big favours. She's done both of us several big favours; that she didn't have to do. Because she's a good person. So you can show some respect. Okay? Okay?

KEITH: Yeah. Fine. Whatever.

A moment.

JACKY *notices marks on the door of his fridge.*

JACKY: Was this you?

    Keith

    Was this you on the fridge?

KEITH: I don't know—what is it?

JACKY: Dirty marks all over my fridge door

KEITH: Wasn't me

JACKY: Well, who else would it be?

KEITH: I dunno

JACKY: Well I do, cos it wasn't me

KEITH: Okay

JACKY: And nobody else lives here. Do they?

    Nobody else puttin' their dirty little hands on my fridge

    He notices something.

Or the walls. Jesus, Keith. The walls? Why do you need to put your hands on my walls?

    JACKY *is wiping down the wall.*

Honestly, ay. What need is there for you to put your grubby little fingers on my walls?

    JACKY *is wiping.*

KEITH: Okay. I'm sorry

JACKY: Wash your hands

KEITH: I do.

JACKY: I mean now

KEITH: I have. They're clean.

JACKY: Bullshit

KEITH: They are, I washed 'em before

JACKY: Show me

KEITH: Are you for real?

JACKY: When you get your own place you can wipe your hands on the walls. Until then, while you're staying in my house, you can keep 'em to yourself

KEITH: It's not yours yet

JACKY: Show me your hands

    A moment.

    KEITH *walks over to* JACKY.

He holds out his hands.

JACKY *inspects them.*

KEITH: See?

JACKY: Turn them over

KEITH *turns his hands over.*

KEITH: See?

JACKY: Okay

KEITH: See?

JACKY: Yes. I see

KEITH: All nice and clean
Just like you.

SCENE 14: JUST A STORY

GLENN *and* JACKY *are at the work Airbnb.* GLENN *is holding a record gift-wrapped in brown paper.*

GLENN: Wow

JACKY: You don't even know what it is

GLENN: What is it?

JACKY: Open it

GLENN: Now? Should I open it now?

JACKY: Why not?
I hope you don't already have it. I don't think you would

GLENN: It's vinyl?

Laughter.

Obviously—obviously it's vinyl!

JACKY: Yeah, I'd be surprised if you had it

GLENN: Okay—should I open it now? I'll open it now. Should I?

JACKY: Fuck, I dunno. Maybe I'll take it back!

GLENN: No, no. No, no. I'll open it. Thank you, Jacky

GLENN *opens the paper packaging carefully.*

Did you wrap it yourself? Okay, let's …

He takes the record out carefully and looks at it.

JACKY: You don't have it already do you?

GLENN: I've had it before. I've sold it. It's fairly popular

JACKY: But you didn't keep a copy?

GLENN: No, I've never had my own copy, no

JACKY: All the mob back home love Charlie Pride. Laughin', drinkin', fightin', tellin' stories, weddings, funerals, new baby: Country-and-Western

Cryin' music

GLENN: That's right

JACKY: Anyway. I—uh—I hope you like it. It's a bit of a novelty, really. I know you don't really listen to Country-and-Western. But, like you said, it all comes from the blues

GLENN: I love it

JACKY: Really?

That's Mum's favourite album. Of all time

GLENN: Really?

What's your mum's name? Roberta?

JACKY: Roberta. Berty

GLENN: Berty. What's her favourite song?

JACKY: Hah! That's easy. Number four. 'I'm So Afraid of Losing You Again'

GLENN: Oh! You sang it for me

JACKY: Yeah

GLENN: I remember. Your voice has a wonderful tone

JACKY: You think?

GLENN: For sure. Absolutely.

JACKY: I never learned to sing

GLENN: Some people don't need to. Some people get it; just get it naturally

JACKY: So you like it?

GLENN: I love it

They kiss.

Mmmm

JACKY: And do you like that?

GLENN: Yep

They kiss.

Moment.

Beat.

Shift to 'play'.

Are you a dirty boy?

You are, aren't you?

JACKY: Yes, sir

GLENN: Yeah, you're a dirty boy

What have you got in your pocket?

JACKY: Nothing, sir

GLENN: Doesn't feel like nothing

You stealing from me, boy? This is my house. What have I told you to do in my house?

JACKY: Show respect

GLENN: Down.

JACKY *kneels before* GLENN.

I'm going to teach you a lesson

JACKY: Yes, boss

GLENN *unbuckles his belt.*

JACKY *moves to undo* GLENN*'s fly.*

GLENN: Not yet. Wait. Shirt off.

JACKY *takes off his shirt.*

Turn around. I'm going to teach you some respect; teach you how to behave when you're in my house. Turn around

JACKY *turns around, his back now to* GLENN, *on all fours or kneeling.*

GLENN *pulls the belt from his own pants.*

Now you listen up. I'm boss around here. You're gunna learn how to behave when you're on my property—

The belt is raised, ready to strike JACKY.

You dirty abo bastard

JACKY: Glenn

GLENN: You call me boss

JACKY: Glenn, that's not going to work

GLENN: Oh, okay, yeah. You want to get up on the bed? On the coffee table? Here, I can tie you to the chair again

JACKY: What did you say? Just now? What did you call me?

GLENN: You like it? I thought it was pretty hot. Just that little bit further, you know? Thought it might put the savage in his place

You don't like it?

JACKY: Like it? No, Glenn, I don't fucking like it. 'Like it'?

GLENN: Hey, sorry, sorry. Okay, sorry

It's just play, Jacky. Fun. A story. A character. I'm just playing a role. Like we always do, babe.

Are you okay?

JACKY: What the hell's wrong with you?

GLENN: Hey, don't shame me. I'm just exploring; exploring what feels good. Like you always say. I take it back. I won't go there again if you're sensitive about it.

Hey. Babe. It's me, Glenn. Come on

Do you not trust me?

JACKY: That was way out of line

GLENN: Okay. Jesus. It was a mistake. I took it back. I didn't mean to hurt you. I apologised

JACKY: I don't do that. I've never done that. It's not part of the package

GLENN: What exactly are we doing here? You just kissed me. You just gave me a record, for God's sake. Your mum's favourite record, Jacky. What am I supposed to make of that?

JACKY: That doesn't give you some kind of … licence to call me whatever you want.

GLENN: It was a mistake. It just came out. You don't have to do it if you don't feel comfortable.

But what are we doing here? We trust each other now

We have something. Something real. Don't we?

Moment.

Just out of curiosity: how much more would it cost, do you think? To call you that?

JACKY: What?

GLENN: Okay! Talk about bringing the mood down. Fuck, Jacky. Maybe next time

JACKY: You should go. I need to go home.

GLENN: Okay

> GLENN *prepares to leave.*

I'm not paying you for this session
JACKY: Excuse me?
GLENN: I'm gunna cancel it—this week's direct debit. I'm not paying.
JACKY: Why not?
GLENN: Well, we haven't done anything
JACKY: We've been here nearly two hours
GLENN: Yeah, but the first ninety minutes was just—
JACKY: Just what?

The first ninety minutes was just what, Glenn?

> GLENN *prepares to leave.*

What are you doing?
GLENN: You told me to leave
JACKY: Not like this. Not without paying me.

Hey. Stop. Answer me. What did you think I was doing for the first ninety minutes of our session, Glenn?
GLENN: What's gotten into you? You're not like this. This isn't you
JACKY: Well who is it then?

> GLENN *leaves.*

SCENE 15: A LITTLE BIT OF CULTURE

Molly O'Brien's Irish Pub, Friday after work.

LINDA *and* JACKY *enter with beers.*

JACKY: Compared to some of the clients I've had lately, Segway is a breeze. I know what's expected of me, you know? No rude surprises. I clock in, I clock out, someone else does all the paperwork and there's the same amount of money in my bank every week
LINDA: Uh-huh
JACKY: I'm wrecked, though. Been taking bookings back to back. Nine to five at the office and then most nights and weekends at the Airbnb. I'm working like a dog. My savings are looking pretty healthy
LINDA: That's good to hear

JACKY: Things are all set for the purchase in July once I go permanent. And I've enrolled at uni too, did I tell you? They took a late application for second semester

LINDA: That's so great.

Jacky, has anyone from Sisterhood mentioned to you anything about an elder passing away? Out east?

JACKY: Pretty sad.

LINDA: Very sad

Aunty Dawn and Sisterhood have dropped right out of contact

JACKY: Yeah, they'll be on sorry business for a little while I'd say

LINDA: How long, do you think?

JACKY: Depends when the funeral is. Depends how senior the elder was. Depends how close they were.

LINDA: Will they be back by tomorrow night?

JACKY: I wouldn't have thought so. Why? Oh, this dinner thing

LINDA: Yes. Yes, this dinner thing

JACKY: They won't be at that

LINDA: Right

JACKY: Is that a big deal?

LINDA: It's a little bit tricky to explain, but it's sort of vital that they're there. There are a couple of people who are really looking forward to meeting them

JACKY: I guess they'll have to meet them another time

LINDA: Okay. It's like this. There are some very wealthy people coming to the event tomorrow night; potential donors who are hopefully going to make a significant contribution to the Communities Program—including to Sisterhood—a very generous contribution that will see us through for the next three years

JACKY: Are we expanding the program?

LINDA: We actually lost our funding. Recently. Very suddenly. It's a long story. I found some money—a lot of money—through some philanthropic partners

JACKY: Where'd you find them?

LINDA: Minerals sector. Mining

Some reps came to an initial prospecting event last weekend

JACKY: The pizza night?

LINDA: And the donors themselves—company executives—have been flown in and put up for tomorrow night's event

JACKY: I thought it was just a get-together

LINDA: It is. It's just that it's also a chance for these donors to meet Sisterhood and the Langhorne family. It's sort of why they're here

JACKY: Why is it so important that they meet the Langhorne family?

LINDA: Because they think they are donating—well they are donating—to a local Aboriginal community cause

The Sisterhood-Communities partnership. The Langhorne family are local and they're also at the centre of Sisterhood. Right?

JACKY: So some mining executives have been flown in to have dinner with some Aboriginal women—

LINDA: Well, that's a slightly reductive way of phrasing it, but—

JACKY: But now there's gunna be no local Aboriginal women at the do?

Did Aunty Dawn mob know about this arrangement?

LINDA: Absolutely

JACKY: And they were into it?

LINDA: We were still ironing a few things out, but yes, as far as I know, and based on our last exchanges, they were more or less in full agreement. But now, according to you, they've just vanished

JACKY: According to me?

LINDA: Sorry. I meant according to what you've told me about how this 'sorry business' works. Can you see we're in a bit of a pickle?

JACKY: So what, if the Langhorne family don't come to this one dinner, you think they might miss out?

LINDA: Everybody's going to miss out

JACKY: Surely it's not that cut and dry

LINDA: Philanthropy is extremely competitive at the best of times. You know that. At this time of year, it's a miracle that I could even get a phone call with a single representative. Let alone organise a prospecting event and then a face-to-face with two mining executives

JACKY: Segway aren't giving the program anything?

LINDA: They'll chuck in the same as they used to, but only if we can secure a significant philanthropic base

JACKY: Yeah, I guess I can see it is a little bit of a pickle

LINDA: Do you think maybe you could—I don't know—try to reach out and see if even one or two of the Langhorne girls could just put in an appearance? Even briefly?

JACKY: It's not really my place to be trying to contact them

LINDA: Yes, no, I—

JACKY: Sorry business is sorry business

LINDA: Of course. I understand

JACKY: I mean, I'll be there on Saturday night. You still want me to come and speak a bit about the traineeships and do cultural dance, yeah?

LINDA: Absolutely. We'll need every little bit of culture we can get

JACKY: I can bring Keith along again. That's two blackfullahs.

LINDA: That's very helpful. Thanks Jacky. Unfortunately I think that for these donations to be secured, the execs will really need to see someone local, from the Langhorne family itself

JACKY: Can't help you there

Moment.

LINDA: Hey, Jacky, would it be crazy to—it's probably not appropriate. But would you ever consider … ? I mean, how close are you with the Langhornes?

JACKY: Well, I know who they are. I know some of the girls

LINDA: So you sort of are connected in?

To Aunty Dawn, and … It's an extended sort of thing; family, kinship, isn't it? For Aboriginal people?

JACKY: Do you mean am I a part of the Langhorne family?

LINDA: Well, no, I know you're not. Technically

Did any of them ever tell you how much they were looking forward to the dinner? They really were

JACKY: Are you thinking I could pretend to be a Langhorne?

LINDA: It could really just be a kind of vague representation. Just for the donors. And in all likelihood, we wouldn't even see them again for the next three years

JACKY: Are you serious?

LINDA: It could be just for a moment, you know. It could just be a kind of subtle implication for this very specific purpose with this very specific audience

JACKY: Just explain to the donors that everyone's on sorry business. They'll understand

LINDA: Maybe. Maybe not. Either way, it doesn't look that great

JACKY: If I pretended to be a Langhorne, Aunty Dawn might literally kill me. Not that these donors would probably even know the difference

LINDA: Exactly. Exactly. They wouldn't even know

JACKY: Linda, it's insane

LINDA: Is it? Sisterhood were all set to come. The girls were going to dance and everything. It's just bad timing. I personally think that if it was me, I'd want my group to be funded. Wouldn't you? You probably wouldn't even have to mention it to them

KEITH *approaches with an armful of beer glasses.*

Keith!

KEITH: How yas goin?

LINDA: Never better. How's your shift? They've got you working on the bar now, I see

KEITH: Kitchen hand, too, sometimes

LINDA: Moving up in the world

KEITH: Better than being stuck on dishes

Thanks for putting in a good word

LINDA: What are friends for?

KEITH *leaves.*

You're probably right

JACKY: It's just not something I can do

LINDA: Of course. I understand. It's a big ask. And it is kind of crazy.

What a shame that for us to lose out. You've worked so hard to top up your savings. You've enrolled in uni. You're so close to securing the loan on your place. You've done all the right things

JACKY: What's it got to do with me?

LINDA: What do you mean?

JACKY: I mean what's this situation got to do with my job? My course? My loan? My apartment?

LINDA: The funding for the Communities Program is where your traineeship comes from. It's where all the traineeships money comes from. Segway cut the Communities Program.

JACKY: Including my job?

LINDA: I thought I'd made that clear

JACKY: No.

LINDA: Without this private investment, Jacky, there's no full-time contract

SCENE 16: ON BEHALF

Saturday night.

Segway staff, communities and families have gathered in a large function room for a dinner event with Segway board members, philanthropic reps and potential donors.

LINDA *stands to address the gathering.*

LINDA: Well! I hope you all enjoyed that beautiful meal. I'd like to thank you all for coming tonight. We're so proud of our Communities Program and of what we've all accomplished together. It's wonderful to see so many familiar faces, as well as some new faces too. Some of you have come a long way to be here. So thank you. And welcome.

Two years—can you believe it? We're so proud of our Communities program and of what we've all accomplished together. Ourarts-and-crafts initiative, the school-to-work support scheme, our childcare service, language classes, the wildly popular Culture in the Park event. And of course our amazing Segway Women's Community Choir. Weren't they spectacular? Give them another round of applause.

GLENN *enters with a glass of champagne. He is a little drunk.* LINDA *does not see him.*

And of course we're very proud indeed to announce our partnership with Sisterhood, and to welcome them into the Communities Program

KEITH *enters quietly and takes a seat.* LINDA *does not see him.*

Sisterhood is a fantastic grassroots organisation providing support, training and care to imprisoned Aboriginal women and their families. We're so thrilled and grateful to be working closely with Aunty Dawn Langhorne and the extended Langhorne family.

Applause.

Now. Our Indigenous Traineeship Initiative selects and supports outstanding up-and-coming Indigenous professionals, providing them with full-time paid training, as well as support for further professional development

And it gives me great pleasure now to introduce to you one of the shining stars of our Indigenous Traineeship Initiative—Jacky—who is going to tell you all a bit more about it. And about himself. And his culture. Jacky is a great contributor to our program and a proud representative of this city's rich and vibrant Indigenous community

JACKY *emerges, dressed smartly, but also partially adorned in culturally significant garb.*

He does not see GLENN *or* KEITH.

JACKY: Ah, g'day everyone. Good evening. So yeah, my name's Jacky. I'd like to start by acknowledging, like we always do, this country, and by paying respect to our elders. Aunty Dawn and most of the Langhorne family unfortunately couldn't make it tonight due to some last-minute cultural commitments. I'll say more about that in a moment.

I've only been working with the Communities Program for a little while; but I can already tell that it's a great partnership that does great things in the community for a whole range of people who really benefit; who really need them. We all need access to the kinds of things that the Communities Program provides. Like Linda always says, and as we all know, a good life starts with family and community and access to meaningful work.

I was recently fortunate to have been invited into Segway's Indigenous Traineeship Initiative. I wasn't sure I'd ever be able to return to my degree after a few rough years where I wasn't studying. And I'd sort of given up trying to get myself work in my chosen field. This opportunity to get back into a career and back to study has really helped me take a step closer to realising a more secure future for myself. And for my family

As I said, Aunty Dawn and the sisters couldn't be here this evening. We, unfortunately, sadly, lost an important elder last week. Out East. So yeah, a lot of people in our Community—in our family—are out on sorry business at the moment, which is an important cultural responsibility.

My sisters over at Sisterhood are a great team of strong, community-minded women. It's my privilege to work alongside my sisters as local Aboriginal leaders, and to work with Segway towards common goals. In the spirit of Reconciliation.

And so I'm proud to be able to say on behalf of Sisterhood and Aunty Dawn, and on behalf of the local mob, and as a member of the Langhorne family, that we really appreciate the opportunity and the generous financial support to work together going forwards. Thank you.

Applause.

JACKY *begins to remove his shirt.*

Now; I'd like to share with youse all a bit of culture.

He maintains an engaging patter as he undresses.

I'll try to get a move on cos it's pretty cold up here. I've just been up north for a bit. That warm humid weather does wonders for your skin, I tell ya. You probably reckon I'm about twenty-five! I'm fifty-five!

Laughter.

Now shirtless, he has some ochre on his chest.

Nah, just joking. But you know what they say: black don't crack!

Matter of fact, the other day one white lady said to me 'geeze, you got nice skin! Do you use Oil of Ulan?' I said to her: 'Isn't it oil of mylan.' She said 'Oil of *my*lan?' I said 'Ay. It's not your land, it's *my* land'

Laughter.

I said 'No, sister, I'm only jokin' around; this here is a time of—a time of reconciliation and harmony and, you know, living together, cooperating and all that … it's oil of *our*land'

Laughter, including from LINDA, *as* JACKY *prepares to perform.*

So yeah, welcome everyone. Great to see you all. Enjoy your night and I look forward to speaking with youse later on. I'm gunna finish up with a cultural dance from our mob

KEITH *is gone.*

SCENE 17: JOB WELL DONE

A little later. JACKY *stands fully dressed as* LINDA *approaches with two glasses of champagne.*

LINDA: Brilliant. Everyone loved it. That was exactly what we needed.

> *She offers* JACKY *a glass.*

Go on. Job well done.

> JACKY *accepts the glass and takes a small, polite sip.*

No sign of Keith in the end?

JACKY: He had to work. And I did sort of subtly encourage him to give this one a miss

LINDA: Right. Now, one more thing—sorry—we really should just pop over and speak to these donors; really bury this thing. They're dying to meet you and now they've had a couple of drinks, it's a great time to butter them up

> GLENN *is approaching with a glass of champagne, visibly drunker than before. Neither* LINDA *nor* JACKY *see him.*

I know this couldn't have been easy. Thank you for playing along

> LINDA *hugs* JACKY.

> GLENN *is now close and* LINDA *sees him.*

Oh. Hi Glenn. Nice to see you. I wasn't sure whether you'd come

GLENN: Good evening

> JACKY *sees* GLENN.

LINDA: Glad you could make it. Jacky, this is my old friend—

GLENN: Old former husband friend

LINDA: Glenn

> *A moment.*

JACKY: Nice to meet you, Glenn

GLENN: That was—ah—some performance you gave us before

LINDA: Brilliant wasn't it

GLENN: Yeah … it was really … I don't know … something else

JACKY: Glad you enjoyed it

LINDA: Love to catch up in a moment, Glenn, we're just on our way to speak to the donors, so—

GLENN: What is this?

LINDA: What is what?

JACKY: It's a dinner

GLENN: Come on, what is all this? This is the new job, is it?

LINDA: Do you two know each other?

JACKY: No

GLENN: Yes

JACKY: I think Glenn might have me mistaken for someone else

GLENN: Yes, we do know each other. Or at least we did, until recently; knew one another rather intimately

JACKY: Glenn was a—

GLENN: A what?

JACKY: He was a—

GLENN: Go on?

JACKY: Glenn was a client of mine

GLENN: A client. I was a client, was I?

LINDA: Right

JACKY: Yeah

LINDA: Okay.

That makes sense

Well, Glenn, Jacky and I happen to work together as well

GLENN: Of course—Segway's shining star!

LINDA: And we've got a couple of people to speak to, just now, so /

GLENN: / The model Indigenous trainee for Linda's precious Communities Program /

LINDA: / Okay, Glenn /

GLENN: / The poster boy for Linda's great big expansive vision

LINDA: That's quite enough

JACKY: Take it easy, Glenn

GLENN: Take it easy? Take it easy?

LINDA: Yes. Take it easy before you humiliate yourself—

GLENN: Humiliate myself?

LINDA: And ruin a very special event. Sorry, Jacky, this is most embarrassing

GLENN: Embarrassing? Who's embarrassed?

LINDA: This is not the time or the place for any of your bullshit

GLENN: Are you embarrassed, Jacky? Linda? You don't look embarrassed

LINDA: I'm extremely embarrassed, Glenn

GLENN: Of what? Of me? And my 'racist little fantasy'

LINDA: For god's sake, it's none of my business what you get up to in your own time

GLENN: Or are you worried that I'm going to cause a scene before your donors get a chance to meet your one black employee?

LINDA: Does this place have any kind of security, because I think it's time for you to / go now, Glenn

GLENN: / Oh, security, security! Secure the premisis!

JACKY: Here, look, I can just /

> JACKY *moves to begin to escort* GLENN.

GLENN: / How dare you put your hands on me

JACKY: Come on, Glenn, let's get you home

LINDA: Thank you, Jacky. Yes, show Glenn out, please, if you wouldn't mind

GLENN: Don't you fucking touch me, you animal

> GLENN *shrugs* JACKY *off.*

Get off.

[*To* LINDA] I hope you really just … enjoy your renewed, expanded program. And your promotion. And your renovations.

LINDA: Oh, piss off, Glenn

GLENN: [*to* JACKY] I thought you were from 'up north'. Huh? 'The mish'? Mum? Bubba Ruby-May? Why this whole charade week after week?

JACKY: My life is none of your business

GLENN: Clearly. Clearly your life—whatever that even is—is now Linda's business. Obviously you're just some kind of performing fucking monkey

[*To* LINDA] Helping Linda fund her 'Aboriginal Community Organisation'.

LINDA: Bubye, Glenn

GLENN: You manipulative, two-faced bitch.

I'll show myself out

> GLENN *leaves.*

SCENE 18: FLESH AND BLOOD

Later, JACKY *sits at Molly's with a jug of beer. He nurses a half-empty glass, moderately drunk.*

KEITH *enters and approaches* JACKY.

JACKY: How was your shift? Have a seat

KEITH: Are you drunk?

JACKY: Not yet. Siddown

KEITH: You're drunk

JACKY: So what if I am? What.drinking beer, getting drunk at the pub—that's against the law now is it?

KEITH: I don't know what's goin on with you, but you better pull your head in

JACKY: You know what is against the law? Stealing from ones employer

KEITH: What are you talking about?

JACKY: I just saw Craig and Mary. You know—the owners of this pub? Don't worry, they're gone now. But they told me all about the roast

KEITH: What roast?

JACKY: Sunday roast. Sorry—'Thursday roast'. Keith's big deadly Thursday roast. With peas, potatoes, pumpkin, carrots how Mum does 'em? They showed me the footage. Of you. Goin' in the kitchen, openin' the prep fridge, takin' out that big , lovely lamb roast. And the pumpkin, and the potato, peas and carrots, jug of gravy, mint jelly. Chuckin' it all in a Coles bag and takin' it. Just takin' it.

KEITH: It's just a fuckin' roast

JACKY: What is wrong with you?

KEITH: It was just one gammon little roast. There was like a hundred roasts in there

JACKY: Do you know how much each of those lamb roasts costs?

KEITH: They can take it out my pay. Like my uniform and all my meals.

JACKY: That leg of lamb gets cut into fifteen portions. And each of those portions goes on a plate with potatoes, pumpkin, chips, salad, gravy. A thirty-dollar plate

KEITH: I know, I make them with my own hands

JACKY: Well do you know how to multiply thirty dollars by fifteen, Keith? Can you figure that out? Or are you too much of a dumb fuck? When four hundred and fifty dollars' worth of stock goes missing, Keith, the owners of a business notice. They care. They investigate. They have cameras

KEITH: Four hundred and fifty dollars? They buy them legs of lamb in bulk for like twelve bucks each. It's just raw meat when we get it. And that was about two dollars' worth of veggies and a spoonful of gravy powder. Thirty bucks is the price they slap on the plate after we make it

JACKY: So that makes it okay to steal?

KEITH: They make a fortune off them plates. Who cuts the potatoes and pumpkin? Peels 'em? Makes the salad? Who mixes the gravy? Cleans the bain-marie? Cleans the pans? The whole oven? The whole kitchen? Me. Or one of the other kitchen hands. Last Sunday the head chef was hungover and he never even come, so I even had to prep the roasts, then roast 'em, and then cut 'em up and serve 'em myself

Did Craig and Mary's cameras see that, too? Or did their cameras see my missing Sunday rates?

JACKY: Running a pub is hard work. Managing staff, rosters, managing people, payroll; it's not a perfect science. People make mistakes sometimes. But they do their best

KEITH: They do pretty well if you ask me

JACKY: Good for them. They're good people running an honest business. They've got a young family and they run a good simple pub. Stealing from them is stealing from their kids

KEITH: Not paying properly is stealing from me

JACKY: They pay the legal rate

KEITH: They pay what that can get away with. And even when they do pay the legal rate, it's fuck all compared to what they make off us

JACKY: Craig and Mary aren't some kind of evil overlords. As far as bosses go, they're pretty bloody good. And they are my friends. This place is like my second home. They've given you a chance, a good chance. And what do you do in return? You go and shit on their dinner table, you selfish prick

I wasn't in a good place when I got to Melbourne. Between Mary and Craig and Linda, I got some help to get on my feet. And not sorry-way. Not pity-way. They gave me good honest work. I needed a chance, an opportunity. And they gave it to me

And now I have to sit in their bar, while they tell me straight to my face that my own brother—my own flesh and blood—stole from them

KEITH: I'm your flesh and blood, am I? You sure about that? Is Laila? Is Bubba Ruby? Is Mum?

You sure you're not a Langhorne?

Silence.

JACKY: I thought you had work tonight

KEITH: They didn't need me

JACKY: How much did you see? I know it wasn't ideal

KEITH: Ideal?

JACKY: It's complicated

KEITH: So explain. Go on, then. Or am I too much of a dumb fuck to understand?

JACKY: Segway's board cut all the funding for the Communities Program at the last minute. Linda already promised all this money to Sisterhood as part of their partnership so she went and found some money through some mining company donors—philanthropists. Heaps of money. Sisterhood and Aunty Dawn were into it but then they suddenly had to go for sorry business and couldn't come and meet the donors. And the donors needed to see that the funding was going to go to local mob. Or they wouldn't have handed it over. Okay?

KEITH: You forgot the part where you get the big money

JACKY: —

KEITH: And the part where you get to buy a house

JACKY: Come on. Keith

KEITH: And the part where you pretend to be someone you're not, from somewhere you're not, and use another mob's name, and claim another mob's country, and speak on behalf of another mob's senior fuckin' elders

JACKY: Keith, come on, listen /

KEITH: / No you listen, Jacky.

You think it's a game? Do you? You think you can just run around like Linda's little dog, gettin' fed scraps off the mining-money table, and climbin' her ladder—and get away with it?

JACKY: I wasn't just climbing the ladder. The Communities Program is important. A lot of ordinary people will suffer without it. Okay, so I stretched the truth a little bit to butter up a couple of billionaires

KEITH: Stretched the truth? Bruss you sold them the skin off your own back

JACKY: I didn't want to do it. It needed to be done. It's not the end of the world. Sisterhood need that money

KEITH: Obviously they don't need it enough to fuck with black protocols. You gonna get yourself in some serious trouble

JACKY: Well, that's my business, isn't it?

KEITH: Wrong. That's my business. That's our whole family's business. You gonna get our whole family in serious fuckin' trouble if you don't pull your head in very fuckin' soon.

Bruss, you wanna have a good hard look at yourself. I was proper shame tonight. Sittin' there watchin' you do that

And then doin' our mob's dance. Tellin' our mob's stories, sharin' our culture. I couldn't even look at you

JACKY: I learned our culture at home on our country. Just like you. I got every right to share it. That's what them old fullahs taught us

KEITH: When them old fullahs taught us that stuff, it wasn't so we could just run around doin' it whenever, wherever, for whoever. All them dances and songs—our culture: it's meant to keep us connected to our own country, not help you help yourself to someone else's. Our stories, our history and knowledge: that's real shit. It means something. You don't just give it away. It's not just another show for rich cunts to buy

And even that joke! 'Oil of ulan? Oil of mylan? Oil of our land?' That's not even your joke. That's Sean Choolburra's joke.

Do you have anything at all that's actually yours? That's actually real?

The mob up home? Bruss, they wouldn't even recognise this bloke sittin' in front of me. Mum put Nan in the ground without you. We all did. Bubba Ruby's a year old. What, you can't fly back sometimes? It's not like you got no money.

JACKY: If you love it so much up at the mish, why don't you piss off back there?

KEITH: Maybe I will

JACKY: Good. Cos I'm sick of the sight of you. I'm sick of your shit all over my house, I'm sick of your filthy marks on my walls, I'm sick of your lazy, entitled attitude. I'm sick of you bludgin' money and pissin' it up the wall. I'm even sick of the smell of you, stinkin' up my loungeroom. So why don't you fuck off back to the mish where you belong with all the other—

KEITH: The other what?

JACKY: I want you to go back to the apartment

KEITH: The other what?

JACKY: And clear out

KEITH: This is how they do it

JACKY: Tonight

KEITH: They pick one, and they go to work on him

JACKY: Before I get home

KEITH: Yeah? And where am I supposed to go?

JACKY: I don't care. Sleep in a park under a tree. Sleep under a bridge. Just pack your shit, get out of the apartment and get on the first train in the morning goin' north.

Go on, get. Before I call the cops on you

KEITH: For what?

JACKY: For stealing from good, hard-working, law-abiding people

KEITH: White people

JACKY: My people

KEITH: You really got it all sorted out now, don't ya. Good job, good house, good money, good friends. You're really in a good place. You don't even have to suck cock for it no more. Yeah. You think I don't know? You think that I think that you coulda saved up enough money for a deposit on an apartment just from workin' in a pub and doin' part-time cultural dance work?

You got no shame, ay. You got no shame suckin' dick and sellin' your ring. Honest to god, that makes me full shame for you. I heard you was doin' that in Sydney, but I thought people musta just been stirrin'.

You're just anyone and everyone's sexy black poster boy. Well I hope you enjoy whatever you buy with your white cock money. And your gammon communities-program-mining-company-reconciliation-Jacky-Jacky-hush-money

And I hope Aunty Dawn sorts you out for that shit tonight. Properly

JACKY: Aunty Dawn doesn't have to know

KEITH: Aunty Dawn already knows

JACKY: —

KEITH: Because I already told her

JACKY: You what?

KEITH: You heard me

> KEITH *stands.*

What kind of blackfulla are you?

> KEITH *leaves.*

> JACKY *sits.*

> *A while.*

> *He pours himself a beer and drinks; slowly at first, then all at once.*

> GLENN *arrives and watches as* JACKY *pours another glass, draining the jug. He drinks.*

> GLENN *approaches. He is drunk, a little unsteady on his feet.*

> *A moment.*

GLENN: I'm so sorry for before. I really don't know what got into me. I've been—I'm a bit of a mess lately

JACKY: It's not a great time, unfortunately, Glenn

GLENN: I shouldn't have said those things about you and about Linda. It was way out of line. It was just quite a shock for me. Seeing you together. That's all. A shock.

Quite a coincidence, don't you think?

JACKY: Sure, yeah

GLENN: I'm sorry

JACKY: Thank you

GLENN: I've really been feeling—

JACKY: Glenn

GLENN: No, no, hear me out, hear me out. I've been feeling bad. I feel bad. I've been feeling really bad. Okay?

JACKY: —

GLENN: Okay? I have. We left on—I left on—well, we parted on a very unfortunate—on a terrible note. I can't stop thinking about it. The

money, especially, the money that I owe you. For our session. It's
not right

JACKY: It's fine

GLENN: It's not. It's not right. You were right. There was so much more
in the sessions than just—you know—the sex part. And of course
I see that now and I think it's only right that I pay you for it—for
that—and I actually—

GLENN searches for his wallet.

Here, look—I actually have money—cash

Finds it.

I actually have it on me right now. I went and got it after I left the
event. I felt so bad and I wanted to go back and pay you, but when
I got back everyone was gone and—

JACKY: Glenn, it's really not the time or place to—

GLENN begins to count out money.

GLENN: And I've actually been looking for you. And I've got it, so—
let's see

He counts it out.

Here, I'll chuck in some extra—interest, a bonus. Fifty extra. Make
it a hundred. Two. There

Money sits on the table.

It's the least I can do.

JACKY: Thanks

GLENN: Do you want to count it?

JACKY: I trust you

Beat.

GLENN: You've been so good to me

JACKY: Glenn, I really need you to—

GLENN: You have. You're amazing, Jacky. You are, you know?

JACKY: I've got a lot on my plate and I've got some family problems
at the moment, so—

GLENN: You've been—you've saved my—you've changed my life,
Jacky. You know that?

JACKY: I'm really glad to hear that, really, I am.

Thank you for the money.

Beat.

GLENN: Will you be with me again?

JACKY: I don't think that's a good idea

GLENN: I want to be with you. I need to be with you, Jacky

He sings.

Jack-Jack-Jacky

JACKY: Glenn.

GLENN: Jacky—I love you, Jacky

JACKY: —

GLENN: I love you, Jacky. Do you love me?

JACKY: —

GLENN: Come on. You love me too, don't you?

JACKY: No. I'm sorry. I don't

GLENN: Then how come you did all of that stuff with me?

JACKY: Because you paid for it, Glenn. 'Boyfriend Experience.' Roleplay? Remember? You were a client—just one client out of I don't even know how many—dozens. It was an exchange. You needed what you needed. I needed what I needed. We both got what we needed. Win-win

GLENN: You kissed me. You said you don't kiss

JACKY: I chucked it in. A bonus

Beat.

GLENN: I thought you didn't drink.

JACKY: I think it's best for you to go

GLENN: You're drunk now

JACKY: You're drunk

GLENN: I didn't fucking say I wasn't

Look at you sitting on a barstool drinking alone in this shithole dive

You're no different

JACKY: Excuse me?

GLENN: You're no different. You're no better than the rest

JACKY: The rest of what?

GLENN: Parading around in your nice suit. Your earrings. Your clean, pressed shirt. Your clean, clear skin. Your slicked-back hair. Your satchel. Like you've got somewhere to be. Like you're going somewhere. Like you matter

JACKY: Fuck you

GLENN: Like you matter. Like you're better than any other abo drinking on the street; sitting in the park. Like you're better than them. All that … lot. You're just a drunk. And a whore. A whore too.

I don't owe you shit

Beat.

GLENN *starts crying.*

I'm sorry, I'm sorry. Oh, god, I'm so sorry. I didn't mean it—I didn't mean any of it. I did it again. Fuck. God I'm such a wreck—look at me, I'm drunk again. I'm so drunk.

I'm such a mess without you.

I *love* you, Jacky

JACKY: If you love me so much—

GLENN: Yes, yes I do—

JACKY: Then what I want—

GLENN: Yes? What do you want?—

JACKY: More than anything—

Is for you to leave me alone

GLENN *sniffles and pulls himself together somewhat.*

GLENN: You're right.

You are. You're right. I've paid what I—I've settled things between us.

He places the money back on the table.

I should go. Shouldn't I? I shouldn't have interrupted you like this and—

I'll go now. Okay?

JACKY: Bye, Glenn

GLENN: Bye, Jacky

GLENN *leaves.*

A moment.

JACKY *puts the money in his pocket.*

He stands and takes his glass and jug to the bar.

SCENE 19: SORRY

The next morning in Jacky's apartment, JACKY *is asleep in his clothes on the couch. He wakes slowly and looks around, hungover. The place is a mess and there are empty bottles on the floor. Keith is gone.*

Jacky's phone rings. He peers at it, takes a deep breath and answers.

JACKY: Hi Aunty Dawn

> *He listens stiffly for some time.*

Yep

> *He listens, swallows.*

Yep

> Yep, for sure

> *He listens, struggles and nods.*

Okay

> Yep.
> Okay, Aunty Dawn.
> Sorry Aunty Dawn.
> Okay.
> Bye

> JACKY *hangs up. He notices something in his pocket and pulls out the money that* GLENN *gave him. He puts it on the table.*

SCENE 20: JUST A ROAST

A short time later.

LINDA *arrives.*

LINDA: Is now a bad time?

> I tried to call

> LINDA *comes in.*

> I brought you a coffee

JACKY: Thanks

LINDA: So, this is the place. It's nice. Keith around?

JACKY: He went out

LINDA: Look, it's none of my business, whatever you and Glenn have been doing. Okay? I'm not—I really couldn't care less. But I'm just so so sorry that it had to come out last night like that

JACKY: It's okay

LINDA: He's a very troubled man. That's no excuse. He's a very kind man, deep down. Very loving

JACKY: I know

LINDA: But he is troubled. Anyway, it's none of my business. I just wanted to say—again—that I'm sorry. And deeply ashamed of his behaviour.

I also came to tell you some good news. You remember the second donor? The older gentleman? He was really very impressed

JACKY: With what?

LINDA: With you. And with the program in general. But really, he loved meeting you and hearing your story. He made an informal pledge straight after the event. I got the official email first thing this morning

JACKY: What did he say?

LINDA: He said you were just the kind of individual that his company's looking to support. They want to work closely with you to develop your career. They want to quadruple our Indigenous traineeships. And they want to take care of the Communities Program for the next three years. Your contract and your study, your loan—they're gonna be fine

JACKY: What about the other donor?

LINDA: He wasn't quite so interested. Would have liked to have met the Langhorne girls, I think

JACKY: Did Aunty Dawn call you?

She called me. Just now

LINDA: And what did she say?

JACKY: What do you think?

LINDA: Well, I wouldn't know, because she hasn't spoken to me since Tuesday last week, has she?

JACKY: I don't think Sisterhood are going to be working with Segway any more

LINDA: Well that's a shame. They know best, I suppose.

Jacky, I used to be part of a little women's advocacy group. The Inner North Working Women's Centre. Very principled. Very tenacious. Very broke.

When we lost our measly bit of funding, we had to decide: do we double down, or do we bite the bullet; make some strategic compromises? I held the hard line, fought to stay independent; no corporate ties. And we did, we stayed 'true'. And we went under; ran out of money, collapsed. We couldn't pay our rent, we lost our office, the group fractured and split. We stopped providing one set of services, then another. Then another.

It's good to have principles. I still do. But at some point you grow up. You stop clinging to some abstract, perfect, 'correct' ideal about how the world 'should' be. Because ultimately we need to get shit done. Here and now. And you need money for that. And it's got to come from somewhere. Right?

What else did Aunty Dawn say?

JACKY: She fuckin' tore me a new one

LINDA: Did she? Did she really?

JACKY: I had it coming

LINDA: What a load of crap.

Jacky, last night was very nearly an appalling waste of everybody's time and limited resources, and an appalling waste of the very hard-to-find and even-harder-to-leverage goodwill of serious philanthropists. And you prevented it from being just that.

JACKY: I misrepresented a senior elder on her own country

LINDA: They wouldn't send one person. Not one single representative of their entire family to secure a very handsome sum of money for the future of their program

JACKY: That was Aunty Dawn's mother that passed away

LINDA: And I'm very sorry to hear it. But life goes on. I lost my father last August. We didn't all shut our lives down.

I mean come on, Jacky. You and I—look at me—you and I both know that it's absolutely absurd that all of the vulnerable families that our program serves—all of those migrant families and single working mothers that rely on our program—should have to miss out on that money and those services because the special and particular cultural preferences of some negligibly small minority of people prevented them from coming to the event they'd already fucking committed to weeks in advance

JACKY: Sorry business is sorry business

LINDA: Sorry business, sorry business, sorry business.

You know who's sorry? Me. Sorry that Sisterhood and the Langhornes are too caught up in their own seperate business to answer the phone and take care of some *actual* business that I had already done all the legwork for

I don't know about you, but that doesn't strike me as being particularly committed to getting things done in the real world

JACKY: Thanks for coming to let me know about the funding

LINDA: Thanks for doing your bit. Like a grown-up

Beat.

I should get out of your hair. I've gotta get down the coast and meet the plasterer about the new walls. I just wanted to come and let you know the good news

JACKY: I thought you lived nearby

LINDA: I do. The renos are on my other place.

Jacky, you did the right thing. I'll see you tomorrow?

LINDA *leaves.*

JACKY *is alone for some time. He cleans and tidies half-heartedly.*

KEITH *appears.*

KEITH: There was a train at nine but my pay's not in the bank yet. I called Laila for a loan, told her you kicked me out and sent me back to the mish. She's broke till Thursday. She told me to come back here and sort things out

JACKY: Where'd you sleep?

KEITH: In the park

JACKY: Weren't you cold?

KEITH: Yep.

JACKY: Sorry

KEITH: I'm sorry I stole the roast. If the cops come, can you talk to 'em with me? I don't wanna get in trouble. And you can talk to cops. I remember one time on the mish they come round and they was hassling dad and you talked to 'em and they just left. Remember?

JACKY: Yeah, I remember

KEITH: How do you do that? Cops never listen to us

JACKY: I haven't been through a lot of what you mob have. I know how it all works—all this. The cops aren't gonna come round, bruss

KEITH *begins to tidy with* JACKY.

Aunty Dawn called me this morning

KEITH: Was it bad?

JACKY: It wasn't good. Something had to happen

KEITH: What are you gunna do now?

JACKY: What do you mean?

KEITH: You gunna keep doing that work?

JACKY: Sex work? Or working for Segway?

KEITH: I dunno. Either. Both. What's it like? The sex stuff

JACKY: You really want to know? People think it's all about having crazy sex all night, being some kind of machine, you know? And that is a part of the job. But really most of the actual work is about listening to people and making them comfortable. Being patient, not judging them. Having fun with them. And caring

KEITH: Pay's good too, or what?

Gentle laughter.

JACKY: Pretty good

KEITH: You got a boyfriend or something?

JACKY: Nah. No time

KEITH: Cos you know I don't care, really, that you're like gay or whatever

JACKY: Thanks Keith

KEITH: I don't. And I'm sorry I said that stuff about your work. Really, I don't care. That's your business. And no-one up home cares. Don't worry, I didn't tell no-one. I just know they wouldn't

Beat.

I talked to Mum, too. On the phone

JACKY: She okay?

KEITH: She sounded tired. She asked when you comin' home. She always asks.

KEITH *sees the pile of cash on the table.*

Fuckin' hell. What's this from?

JACKY: You don't wanna know

KEITH: Hey, I wanted to give you some money too

JACKY: For what?

KEITH: For all the bills and, like, I missed some rent

JACKY: Nah, nah

KEITH: Yeah, I feel bad, you know, cos you're saving for the apartment

JACKY: You can't even afford a train ticket

KEITH: When my pay comes through, I mean

JACKY: That's your wages. You keep it

KEITH: You sure?

JACKY: Yeah. Put it on a horse

They keep cleaning.

KEITH: So how much is that on the table, anyway?

JACKY: Probably enough for us to get home

KEITH: Ay?

JACKY: What you reckon?

KEITH: You serious? For what? A visit? Or stay for a bit?

JACKY: I dunno. See what happens

KEITH: What about your new job?

JACKY: I don't think it's for me

KEITH: So what about the apartment?

JACKY: It's just an apartment

KEITH: What about Linda?

JACKY: Bruss, fuck Linda. Let's go home

KEITH: I'm tellin' Mum

JACKY: Nah, nah

KEITH: Ay?

JACKY: Let's surprise her

KEITH: Yeah. Yeah, mad!

JACKY: Don't tell Laila either

KEITH: Nah, nah, I won't. You never even seen Bubba Ruby, ay?

JACKY: Let's get her a present, too, ay?

KEITH: That's mad, bruss

They've tidied up.

KEITH *handles the cash.*

Oi, I should go pay Molly's. For the roast. Or what? And I'll pay you back out of my wages

JACKY: Don't worry about it

KEITH: Ay?

JACKY: Fuck 'em. Don't worry 'bout it. It's just a fuckin' roast, brah

THE END

Melbourne Theatre Company

Our Donors

We gratefully acknowledge the ongoing support of our leading Donors.

LIFETIME PATRONS

Acknowledging a lifetime of extraordinary support.

Pat Burke
Peter Clemenger AO and
  The Late Joan Clemenger AO
Greig Gailey and
  Dr Geraldine Lazarus

Allan Myers AC KC
  and Maria Myers AC
The Late Biddy Ponsford
The Late Dr Roger Riordan AM

Maureen Wheeler AO
  and Tony Wheeler AO
Ursula Whiteside
Caroline Young
  and Derek Young AM

ENDOWMENT FUND DONORS

Supporting Melbourne Theatre Company's long term sustainability and creative future.

Leading Gifts

Jane Hansen AO and
  Paul Little AO
The Late Max and the
  Late Jill Schultz
The University of Melbourne

$50,000+

The Late Margaret
  Anne Brien
The Late Geoffrey Cohen AM
The Late Biddy Ponsford
Andrew Sisson AO and
  Tracey Sisson
The John & Myriam Wylie
  Foundation

$20,000+

Robert A. Dunster
Prof Margaret Gardner AO
  and Prof Glyn Davis AC

$10,000+

Jane Kunstler

PLAYWRIGHTS GIVING CIRCLE

Supporting the NEXT STAGE Writers' Program.

Louise Myer and Martyn Myer AO, Maureen Wheeler AO and Tony Wheeler AO, Christine Brown Bequest,
Allan Myers AC KC and Maria Myers AC, Tony Burgess and Janine Burgess, Dr Andrew McAliece and
Dr Richard Simmie, Larry Kamener and Petra Kamener

The Ian Potter Foundation | NAOMI MILGROM FOUNDATION | THE MYER FOUNDATION | MALCOLM ROBERTSON FOUNDATION | THE UNIVERSITY OF MELBOURNE

TRUSTS & FOUNDATIONS

Cybec Foundation | The Gailey Lazarus Foundation | HANSEN LITTLE FOUNDATION | The Ian Potter Foundation | NEWSBOYS FOUNDATION

telematics trust | trawalla foundation | JOHN & MYRIAM Wylie | VICTORIA State Government | The Vizard FOUNDATION

Annual giving

Donors whose recent gifts help us enrich and transform lives through the finest theatre imaginable.

BENEFACTORS CIRCLE

$50,000+

The Joan and Peter
  Clemenger Trust
Jane Hansen AO and Paul Little AO

Andrew Sisson AO and
  Tracey Sisson ○ ●

Maureen Wheeler AO and
  Tony Wheeler AO

$20,000+

Paul & Wendy Bonnici
  and Family ●
Krystyna Campbell-Pretty AM ●

Greig Gailey and
  Dr Geraldine Lazarus
Louise and Martyn Myer AO
Anne and Mark Robertson OAM ●

Orcadia Foundation ○
Tania Seary and Chris Lynch ▲
Craig Semple ○

$10,000+

Joanna Baevski ●
Jay Bethell and Peter Smart
The Late Dr Jane Bird ●
Jill Campbell ○
Kathleen Canfell ○
The Cattermole Family
The Cordiner Family ●
Jennifer Darbyshire and
  David Walker
John and Joan Grigg OAM
Linda Herd ●

Amy and Paul Jasper
Petra and Larry Kamener
Daryl Kendrick and
  Leong Lai Peng (Betty)
Suzanne Kirkham
Macgeorge Bequest
Susanna Mason ▲
Ian and Margaret McKellar
McNeilly Family ○
Helen Nicolay ○
Catherine Quealy

Janet Reid OAM and Allan Reid
Lisa Ring
Geoff Slade, Slade Group and
  TRANSEARCH ○
Rob Stewart and Lisa Dowd ●
Helen Sykes ○
Ralph Ward-Ambler AM and
  Barbara Ward-Ambler
Matt Williams – Artem Group
Anita Ziemer ○
Anonymous (2)

$5,000+

John and Lorraine Bates
Marc Besen AC
James Best and Doris Young
Bill Bowness AO
Dr Andrew Buchanan and
  Peter Darcy
Ian and Jillian Buchanan
Bill Burdett AM and Sandra Burdett
Lynne and Rob Burgess
Pat Burke and Jan Nolan
Diana Burleigh
Alison and John Cameron
Ann Cutts
The Dowd Foundation
Prof Margaret Gardner AC and
  Prof Glyn Davis AC
Shane Gild
Charles Gillies and Penny Allen

The Gjergja Family
Roger and Jan Goldsmith
Robert and Jan Green
Lesley Griffin
Fiona Griffiths and
  Tony Osmond ●
David and Lily Harris
Jane Hemstritch AO
Tony Hillery and
  Warwick Eddington
Bruce and Mary Humphries
Sam and Jacky Hupert ●
Dr Sonay Hussein and The Late
  Prof David Penington AC
Jane Kunstler
Glenda and Greg Lewin AM
Martin and Melissa McIntosh
Kim and Peter Monk ●

George and Rosa Morstyn
MRB Foundation
Anne and Jason Murray ●
Tom and Ruth O'Dea ■
Leigh O'Neill ●
Dr Kia Pajouhesh (Smile Solutions)
Bruce Parncutt AO
Christopher Reed
Kendra Reid
Renzella Family
Lynne Sherwood
Tintagel Bay P/L
Marion Webster AM ●
Ursula Whiteside
Janet Whiting AM and Phil Lukies
J & M Wright Foundation
Anonymous (6)

PROGRAM GIVING CIRCLES

▲ **ARTISTIC DIRECTORS**   ○ **PRODUCTION PATRONS**   ■ **YOUTH AMBASSADORS**   ● **WOMEN IN THEATRE**   ● **EDUCATION**

ADVOCATES CIRCLE

$2,500+

Australian Communities
  Foundation – Ballandry
  (Peter Griffin Family) Fund
Angelina Beninati
John G Millard and Andrew Cason
Jenny and Stephen Charles AO
Susanne Dahn
Ann Darby ○ ●
The Dodge Family Foundation
Rodney Dux
Melody and Jonathan Feder ▦
Anna and John Field
Jan and Rob Flew
Nigel and Cathy Garrard
Gaye and John Gaylard
Diana and Murray Gerstman
Heather and Bob Glindemann OAM

Henry Gold
Jane Grover ◆
Jane Hodder ◆
Peter and Halina Jacobsen
Josephine and Graham Kraehe AO
Leg Up Foundation ▦
Alex Lewenberg
Lording Family Foundation
Virginia Lovett and
  Rose Hiscock ○
Prof Duncan Maskell ●
Margaret and John Mason OAM
Don and Sue Matthews
Ging Muir and John McCawley ▦
Sandra Murdoch
Jane and Andrew Murray
Luke and Janine Musgrave

Nelson Bros Funeral Services
Dr Paul Nisselle AM and
  Sue Nisselle
In memory of Marysia and
  Berek Segan AM OBE
Prof Barry Sheehan and
  Pamela Waller
Ricci Swart AM
James and Anne Syme
Richard and Debra Tegoni ●
The Veith Foundation
Kaye and John de Wijn
Price and Christine Williams
The Ray and Margaret Wilson
  Foundation
Gillian and Tony Wood
Anonymous (7)

LOYALTY CIRCLE

$1,000+

Prof Noel Alpins AM and
  Sylvia Alpins
Anita and Graham Anderson ●
Margaret Astbury
Ian Baker and Cheryl Saunders
John and Dagnija Balmford
Prof Robin Batterham
Judy Bourke ●
Steve and Terry Bracks AM
Jenny and Lucinda Brash
Paul and Robyn Brasher
Bernadette Broberg
Nigel and Sheena Broughton
Beth Brown and
  The Late Tom Bruce AM
Dr Douglas and Treena Brown
Nan Brown
Rob and Sal Bruce
Julie Burke
Katie Burke
Pam Caldwell
John and Jan Campbell
Jessica Canning
Clare and Richard Carlson
Fiona Caro
Chernov Family
Keith Chivers and Ron Peel
Assoc Prof Lyn Clearihan and
  Dr Anthony Palmer
Sandy and Yvonne Constantine
Deborah Conyngham ●
Jutta Cowen
Philip Crutchfield KC and
  Amy Crutchfield

Karen and Rachel Cusack ◆
June Danks
Natasha Davies
Megan Davis and Antony Isaacson
Sue and John Denmead
Katharine Derham Moore
Dr Anthony Dortimer and
  Jillian Dortimer
Robert Drake
Mark Duckworth PSM and
  Lauren Moss
Dr Sally Duguid and
  Dr David Tingay
Bev and Geoff Edwards
George and Eva Ermer
Anne Evans and Graham Evans AO
Marian Evans
Dr Alastair Fearn
Peter Fearnside and
  Roxane Hislop
Peter and Mary Fildes
Grant Fisher and Helen Bird
Rosemary Forbes and Ian Hocking
Bruce Freeman ▦
Dr Justin Friebel and Jessica Rose
John R Fullerton
Gill Family Foundation
Ian and Wendy Haines
Charles Harkin
Mark and Jennifer Hayes ●
Luke Heagerty
Sally Heerey and
  The Late Peter Heerey
Diana Heggie ●

Lorraine Hendrata
Kerri Hereward
Emeritus Prof Andrea Hull AO
Nanette Hunter
Ann and Tony Hyams AM
Will and Jennie Irving
Peter Jaffe and Judy Gold
Ben Johnson
Ed and Margaret Johnson
Sally and Rod Johnstone
K and B Jones
Leah Kaplan
Irene Kearsey and Michael Ridley
Malcolm Kemp
Daniel Kilby
Fiona Kirwan-Hamilton and
  Brett Parkin
Doris and Steve Klein
Marianne and Arthur Klepfisz
Larry Kornhauser and
  Natalya Gill ● ▦
Anne Le Huray
Verona Lea
Joan Lefroy AM and
  George Lefroy AM
Alison Leslie
Peter and Judy Loney
Lord Family ◆
Kerryn Lowe and Raphael Arndt
Elizabeth Lyons
Ken and Jan Mackinnon
Karin MacNab
Chris and Bruce Maple
Ian and Judi Marshman

Penelope McEniry
Heather and Simon McKeon ⊠
Garry McLean
Libby McMeekin
Emeritus Prof Peter McPhee AM
   and Charlotte Allen
Rosemary Meagher and
   The Late Douglas Meagher
Melman Trading PTY LTD
Robert and Helena Mestrovic
Ann Miller AM
Ross and Judy Milne-Pott
MK Futures
Barbara and David Mushin ⊚
Sarah Nguyen
Nick Nichola and Ingrid Moyle
David and Lisa Oertle
Susan Oliver AM
Dr Jane and Alan Oppenheim
Arthur Ozols
In loving memory of Richard Park
Dr Annamarie Perlesz
Peter Philpott and Robert Ratcliffe
Philip and Gayle Raftery
David Reckenberg and
   Dale Bradbury

Sally Redlich
Victoria Redwood
Veronica and John Rickard ⊚
Phillip Riggio
Ken Roche ⊚
Roslyn and Richard Rogers
   Family ⊚
Stephen and Sheryle Rogerson
B and J Rollason
Sue Rose
Nick and Rowena Rudge
Jeremy Ruskin and Roz Zalewski
Jenny Russo
Edwina Sahhar
Margaret Sahhar AM
Fiona Scott
Sally and Tim Scott
Jacky and Rupert Sherwood
Diane Silk
Dr John Sime
Pauline and Tony Simioni
Jan and Michael Simon
Tim and Angela Smith
Brian Snape AM
Geoff Steinicke
Dr Ross and Helen Stillwell

Rosemary Stipanov
The Stobart Strauss Foundation
Helene Strawbridge
Suzy and Dr Mark Suss ⊠
Irene and John Sutton
Christopher Swan ⊚
Rodney and Aviva Taft
Elizabeth Tromans
John and Anna van Weel
Valeria Vanselow
Graham Wademan and
   Michael Bowden
Walter and Gertie Wagner ⊚
Kevin and Elizabeth Walsh ⊠
Pinky Watson
Penelope and Joshua White
Ann and Alan Wilkinson ⊚
Ralph Wollner and
   The Hon Kirsty Macmillan SC
Mandy and Edward Yencken
Anonymous (27)

LEGACY CIRCLE

Acknowledging supporters who have made the visionary gesture
of including a gift to Melbourne Theatre Company in their will.

John and Lorraine Bates
Mark and Tamara Boldiston
Bernadette Broberg
Adam and Donna Cusack-Muller
Anne Evans and Graham Evans AO
Bruce Freeman
Peter and Betty Game
Edith Gordon

Fiona Griffiths
Linda Herd
Tony Hillery and
   Warwick Eddington
Irene Kearsey
Dr Andrew McAliece and
   Dr Richard Simmie
Libby McMeekin

Peter Philpott and Robert Ratcliffe
Marcus Pettinato
Jillian Smith
Diane Tweeddale
Anonymous (16)

PROGRAM GIVING CIRCLES

▲ ARTISTIC   ○ PRODUCTION   ▣ YOUTH   ◆ WOMEN IN   ⊚ EDUCATION
   DIRECTORS   PATRONS   AMBASSADORS   THEATRE

Current as of April 2023. For more information about supporting Melbourne Theatre Company
please contact our Philanthropy team at donations@mtc.com.au or visit mtc.com.au/support

Thank you

Melbourne Theatre Company would like to thank the following organisations for their generous support.

Major Partner

Future Directors Initiative Partner

MinterEllison.

Major Marketing Partners

oOh!
unmissable

The Monthly
The Saturday Paper
7am

Presenting Partner

THE LANGHAM
MELBOURNE

Associate Partners

AEGEUS

Frontier
software
Human Capital Management
& Payroll Software/Services

K&L GATES

LITTLE
GROUP

Supporting Partners

COMMITTEE
MELBOURNE FOR

Genovese

THE
LUXURY
NETWORK

QUEST
SOUTHBANK

METROPOLIS
EVENTS

SOH
MELBOURNE

toxi
kitchen

Wilson Parking

Marketing Partners

BROADSHEET

CINEMA
NOVA

invicium
print and beyond

Southbank Theatre Partners

mgc
THE
MELBOURNE
GIN COMPANY

SCOTCHMANS HILL
BELLARINE PENINSULA
VICTORIA
ESTABLISHED 1982

southgate

RRR

Current as of April 2023. To learn more about partnership opportunities at Melbourne Theatre Company or to host a private event, please contact partnerships@mtc.com.au